THE
GEOLOGY
BOOK

by
Dr. John D. Morris

Master
Books

THE GEOLOGY BOOK

Third Printing: March 2004

Printed in the United States of America

Cover Design by Janell Robertson
Interior Design by Brent Spurlock

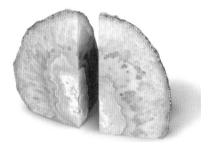

For information write:
Master Books
P.O. Box 726
Green Forest, AR 72638

Please visit our web site
for other great titles:
www.masterbooks.net

ISBN: 0-89051-281-7

Library of Congress: 99-067332

DEDICATION

TO DALTA, CHARA, TIM, AND BETH

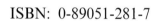

CONTENTS

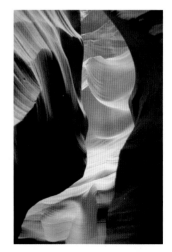

INTRODUCTION

The earth — our home — is a majestic place with a wide variety of things to see and do. Some parts of it are breathtakingly beautiful, other parts less so, but all of the earth is our home.

The Bible tells us that God has given the earth to man as the place where he is to live. A few people have gone to the moon, but that is still part of the earth's system. Someday someone may possibly go into deep space, but the earth is our home. This is where we were born and where we live. God has given it to us to care for and use wisely, for man's good and God's glory.

While we all enjoy the earth as our home, it is also necessary to study it and understand it fully. Scientists observe the earth to learn more about it. Engineers use its materials and farmers make their livelihood from the earth. How can we best gather this information?

Any kind of science, including earth science, is limited to what we can observe. Scientists use their five senses — sight, smell, taste, hearing, and touch — and apply their minds to understand this information.

Sometimes the most interesting thing we can learn about something is its history. How did the earth get this way? What happened in the past before there were people to make observations, to make it the way it is in the present?

Obviously, scientists can't get in a time machine and return to the past to observe the earth in its earlier days. They can only interpret the rocks and fossils and river systems and mountains and all things that exist in the present, and try to discern what the past was like. There are only two basic ways of thinking about the unobserved past, uniformity and catastrophe, and by understanding them we can understand why scientists often disagree. By comparing the two, we can choose which one makes more sense.

The principle of uniformity has a slogan: "The present is the key to the past." By claiming that past processes have been no different from those possible today, some scientists choose to believe that everything happened by gradual processes operating slowly over very long periods of time. For example, the Colorado River carved out the Grand Canyon slowly over 70 million years, they say.

The principle of catastrophe sees evidence that rapid, highly energetic events operated over short periods of time and did much geologic work rapidly. In this view, the Grand Canyon was carved out quickly by huge volumes of water rushing rapidly over the ground. Throughout this book we'll be comparing these two views of earth history, and see which one is better.

Actually, the true history of the earth is given to us in the Bible. We were not here, but God was, and He tells us in the Bible the observations that He made. In fact, He did it all himself.

In the Bible, He tells us that "In the beginning God created the heaven and the earth" (Gen. 1:1). On the earth, He formed the oceans and then the continents, and then He placed plants and living creatures on the earth. Finally, He created man to be His steward of the earth, to keep it and to use it wisely.

In the beginning it was all "very good" (Gen. 1:31) — absolutely perfect — and would have lasted forever. But now we see that the earth is not quite so good. Things go wrong here. There are earthquakes, hurricanes, and natural disasters which destroy everything in their paths. These were not part of the original creation.

What has happened? The Bible answers that question. Adam and Eve rebelled against God, disobeying His commands for them. This, of course, is sin, and there is a penalty for sin. "The wages of sin is death" (Rom. 6:23).

In Adam's day, the penalty for sin was that the entire creation was placed under the curse (Gen. 3:17–21). "Now the entire creation groaneth and travaileth in pain together until now" (Rom. 8:22) due to the presence of sin and its penalty — death.

The Bible also tells us that within a few generations after Adam sinned, sinful man had so multiplied their abuse of the earth and their sinful rebellion against God that God sent the flood to destroy the entire earth. That kind of flood would have totally restructured the entire surface of the globe, and now all the observations that we can make are of a cursed world destroyed by a flood.

As we observe this earth, we still see great beauty and marvelous balance, but we can never fully understand our present earth without knowing its past. Only those who do recognize its true past can make sense out of the evidence that we observe in the present.

As we study the earth, keep these things in mind and try to imagine just how beautiful that created, "very good" earth must have been so that its cursed and destroyed remnant would still be so beautiful.

Chapter 1

PLANET EARTH

Our study of the earth must start with its place in the solar system. It is one of nine planets circling the sun. The inner four planets, including the earth, are solid. The next four planets are much larger than the earth and made entirely of gas. They have no solid material. The outer-most planet, Pluto, is solid once again.

Scientists have sent up probes to Venus and Mars, our nearest neighbors, and found them to be most inhospitable to life. The others are even worse. Mercury is much too close to the sun; it would be too hot to support life. The outer planets are so far from the sun that their temperatures are extremely low. Only the earth is capable of supporting life.

As it revolves around the sun, earth has a slight tilt, giving us the seasons throughout the year. As it rotates on its axis, we have a day and night cycle, each 24 hours.

The earth is the third planet from the sun (above). Along with the other three closest planets, it is made up of solid material. The outer planets such as Saturn (left) are composed entirely of gases, except Pluto.

While many of the planets have moons, their moons are quite small when compared to the planets they circle. Our moon, however, is almost one-quarter the size of the earth and its gravitational pull on the earth is responsible for the daily tides. So many things about the earth make us recognize that it was designed for life — our life — by a wise and powerful God.

The earth is a sphere, rather ball-shaped. Actually, It is a little bit pear-shaped with its diameter at the equator a little larger than its diameter at the poles. For practical purposes, however, we can consider it a sphere, with an average radius of 3,963 miles (6,368 km).

As far as we know, no other planet in the solar system contains water. Necessary for life, the earth has it in abundance, stored primarily in the oceans, which are far deeper, on average, than the continents are high. If the earth's solid material were completely smooth, water would form a worldwide ocean approximately 8,500 feet (2,591 m) deep!

Inside the Earth

On the surface of the earth we see soil, rock, and water, all surrounded by atmosphere. These things comprise only the thin outer skin of the earth. The rest is quite different.

crust, located in the bottom of the Pacific Ocean, but these efforts have not yet been successful. The lower parts of the crust differ from the upper parts, but still we have not directly observed anything other than the crust of the earth.

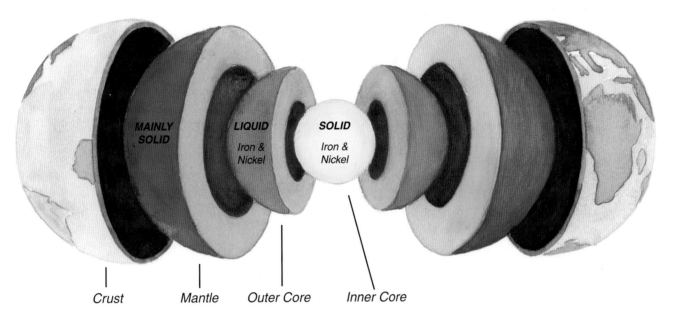

MAINLY SOLID

LIQUID
Iron & Nickel

SOLID
Iron & Nickel

Crust   *Mantle*   *Outer Core*   *Inner Core*

No one has actually drilled deep inside the earth, but by studying the way energy waves travel through the earth, we have a pretty good idea of what is deep inside.

The earth is divided into three main zones. The crust of the earth is the thin outer skin. On the crust are continents and oceans. In some places the crust is at a lower elevation than others, but the difference is very slight compared to the overall size. In fact, if the earth were the size of an orange, and you could hold it in your hand, you would not be able to feel the difference between the highest mountain and the deepest ocean basin.

Efforts have been made to drill through the thinnest part of the

The interior of the earth is made up of four main sections. The crust is very thin and consists of the continents and oceans. The mantle is the largest at 1,900 miles (3,000 km) thick. The outer core is so hot that it is molten liquid, while the inner core is under so much pressure that it is solid.

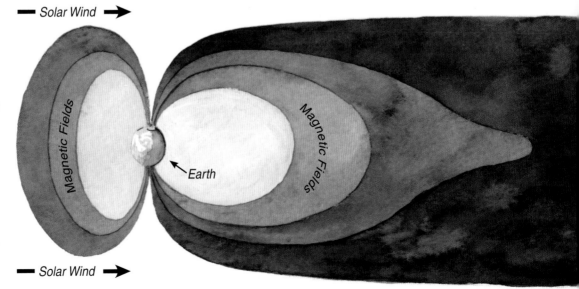

← Solar Wind →

Magnetic Fields

Magnetic Fields

← Earth

← Solar Wind →

The invisible magnetic field around the earth is a result of the earth having an iron core, in much the same way that an iron bar magnet produces a magnetic field.

The crust varies from 3.7 to 6.8 miles (6 to 11 km) thick in the ocean and 15 to 56 miles (25 to 90 km) or so on the continents. Compared to its radius, this is almost like a thin onionskin around the sphere of the earth.

The majority of the earth is made up of the mantle, which is nearly 1,900 miles (3,000 km) thick. The pressures and temperatures inside the mantle are extremely high, but this rock is still in solid form. In general, the mantle is made up of the same sorts of elements as the crust, but with a higher percentage of the elements that pack into more dense minerals.

Scientists have come to suspect that there is a zone in the very uppermost part of the mantle called the asthenosphere. The material here is quite hot and deforms a little more easily than regular rock. In some ways it appears our continental crust actually "floats" on this asthenosphere.

The core of the earth is divided into two zones. Both are made up primarily of the metals iron and nickel, but the outer zone is in molten, liquid form. The pressures and temperatures are intense down there, but the pressures are so great in the inner core that the molten liquid returns to solid form. Even though we only know about them from theory, it does appear that electrical currents flowing in the outer core's conductive metal generate the earth's magnetic field. This is extremely important because the magnetic field shields the earth from harmful radiation coming from the sun and stars. Without it, life would be completely impossible on planet Earth.

The crust can be broken up into plates that seem to "float" on the upper part of the mantle called the asthenosphere. Rifts can occur where the plates come together.

CONTINENTAL Crust

OCEANIC Crust

Asthenosphere

WHY THE EARTH IS UNIQUE FOR LIFE

All life depends on water. If the earth's solid material were completely smooth, it would be covered by water 8,500 feet (2,591 m) deep!

The gravity of the moon pulling on the earth causes the oceans to rise and fall forming the tides.

8

Most earthquakes (colored dots) occur along the edges of the plates (yellow). Volcanoes are also more frequent along these plate boundaries.

The earth is made up of elements that combine together to form minerals which make up rocks. If they combine in a geometric pattern, they form crystals (below).

ASIA
NORTH AMERICA
United States
AFRICA
SOUTH AMERICA
AUSTRALIA
ANTARCTICA
Plate Boundary   Earthquake Depth
shallow ◆ ◆ ▶ ↑ deep

The Crust

Even though the crust is a very minor portion of the total volume of the earth, it is the most interesting. It has the most variety and is, of course, most useful to man. It can be divided into two categories. The continental crust is made up primarily of rocks of granitic composition often covered by sedimentary rock, and the oceanic crust is made up primarily of basaltic rock. Since basaltic rock is more dense than continental granitic rocks, the continents rest at a higher elevation than the oceans. The deeper ocean basins thus contain a vast volume of water, allowing the land surface on which we live to be exposed.

Scientists have long noted that earthquakes tend to occur in certain zones. By plotting the locations of these earthquakes on a map and connecting them with lines, one sees that the crust of the earth is divided up into huge regions called "plates." There are not too many earthquakes on the interior of these plates, but around the edges the earth-quakes tend to occur frequently. Volcanoes also tend to occur on the edges of these plates.

All substances are made up of atoms, or elements. Some are larger, and thus heavier than others. Over 100 different types of atoms and even more varieties of atoms exist on planet Earth; but just a few elements make up the majority of the crust's weight. If we look at those that make up the crust, we see that oxygen dominates, making up almost one-half of its volume. The next is silicon, which is a very common atom in rocks.

The atoms tend to combine into groups called minerals, and it is these minerals which make up rocks. Sometimes these minerals combine in regular geometric patterns forming crystals.

Surrounding the entire crust, of course, is the atmosphere. This provides not only the air that we breathe but a further shield for us from harmful cosmic radiation, and also gives us weather. Because of the atmosphere, we can have rain and usually a blue sky. Without it life would be impossible.

The earth is the perfect distance from the sun to keep it the right temperature, and the earth's tilt causes the seasons.

The atmosphere not only provides air for breathing, but also deflects harmful space radiation and refracts solar radiation.

Chapter 2

The Ground We Stand Upon

The rocks which make up the crust can be divided into three categories based on the processes which formed them. These categories are igneous rocks, sedimentary rocks, and metamorphic rocks.

I. Igneous Rocks

Many rocks in the earth's crust are similar to those which form today by cooling from an original hot, melted condition. These rocks are called igneous rocks from the Latin word *ignis* meaning "fire."

Granite

Massive volumes of a rock called granite make up a large proportion of the continents. Huge granite blocks bulge up, forming the central mass of many mountains. The roots of the continents that extend down into the upper mantle also consist of rocks of granitic composition.

It appears that when God created "the heaven and the earth" (Gen. 1:1), He created a granitic bulk to be the continents. Granite always contains abundant quartz and feldspar with a good bit of mica and hornblende mixed in. A granite-like rock can be formed today by melting a similar rock in a laboratory and

When hot molten lava cools, it forms igneous rocks. Much of the crust is made up of rocks that were once in a melted condition.

allowing it to cool and crystallize once again, under great pressure. "How the granite bodies found everywhere on the continents formed" is the big question. They certainly aren't forming like this today. We do, however, have some evidence that masses of granite could be forming and cooling at depths of between 2 and 5 km under some active volcanoes. They are big, but not continent wide. The molten rock, which evidently forms granite, squeezes up through cracks like toothpaste into the overlying rock where it cools and solidifies fairly rapidly due to the circulation of underground water. Just as the cool water gets heated by the hot rock, so the rock is cooled by the water.

When the molten rock which forms granite erupts onto land, it solidifies as rhyolite. A series of rhyolite lavas was erupted at what is now known as Yellowstone Park. These eruptions were much larger than any observed in modern times. At Yellowstone the hot underground rocks are being cooled by water, which trickles down, gets heated, and returns to the surface as hot springs and geysers.

One common type of rhyolitic volcanic rock is known as obsidian, which almost looks like a chunk of black glass. It is formed by the rapid cooling of lava as it flows on the surface of the ground. This type

In Yellowstone National Park, the volcanic activity that formed the igneous rocks can still be seen in the geysers which erupt hot water and steam.

of rock has been used by Indians for arrowheads, because it fractures in sharp points.

Another common type of igneous rock resulting from eruptions on the land is pumice. This rock is full of air holes due to cooling and thus is very light in weight. Some pieces of pumice actually float on water.

Basalt

Basalt

Most of the world's oceanic crust consists of basalt. Many scientists think molten lava was squeezed up onto the ocean bottom from the upper mantle, where it solidified into solid rock as it cooled. Basalt frequently has abundant pyroxene and plagioclase feldspar, and quite often appears

Obsidian was commonly used by American Indians for arrowheads (above).

Basalt makes up most of the oceanic crust, but can also be found on land. Along the center of the photo can be seen columnar basalts (right).

dark gray or black. Basalt is also found formed by volcanism on land. Often these land-based basalt deposits are incredibly huge, covering hundreds of thousands of square miles in area and are several miles thick. The necessary series of volcanic eruptions which produced these deposits operated on a scale far beyond anything ever witnessed in the modern world.

When a lava flow enters the ocean or a lake, it cools rapidly and takes on the shape of pillows stacked on top of one another. The presence of "pillow lava" helps scientists determine the environment into which a basalt erupted. Pillow lava can be found on the ocean floor, but it can also be found on mountains.

Lava cools rapidly when it enters a body of water, forming "pillow lava," which resembles pillows stacked on top of one another.

II. SEDIMENTARY ROCKS

Among the most interesting types of rocks are the sedimentary rocks. These are the ones which contain most of the world's fossils, petrified wood, and things like that. Most of the world's mountain chains primarily consist of this type of rock, so it forms the cliffs and banks that we see as we drive. Sedimentary rocks are divided into two categories depending on where their materials came from and how they were deposited.

All sediments, by definition, are transported by moving fluids, either water or air. In almost every case the sediments are deposited by water — the ocean or rivers or lakes. Sand deposited by wind in sand dunes is an example of a wind-borne sediment.

Sedimentary rocks are formed underwater into long flat layers. Today, these layers can be seen even in the mountains and canyons.

A. Clastic Sedimentary Rocks

The sediments which make up clastic rocks were derived from previously existing rocks, which were either eroded or broken up, then transported and redeposited somewhere else. Various names are given to clastic rocks depending on the size of the particles which dominate.

Conglomerate

If the grains are bigger than normal sand grains, then the rock is called a conglomerate. The particles which make up the conglomerate may be from pebble-sized up to boulder-sized. In between these larger particles will be smaller sand or clay particles.

In all types of clastic rock, the grains must be bound together by some form of cement. Usually this is a chemical which crystallizes, attaching itself to the adjacent grains. The final rock may be very hard, based on the type of cement, but without the cement the sediments would forever remain unconsolidated and never become a sedimentary rock.

Shale

Shale is the most abundant sedimentary rock made up of cemented particles of clay (and minor silt). These particles are so fine they cannot be seen with the naked eye, but require a microscope to be seen.

Sandstone

If the particles are big enough to be seen, then the rock is called sandstone. Most often, the particles are made up of quartz sand, just like that on most beaches.

Grain Sizes of Clastic Rocks

Particle	Size (millimeters)	Rock
Boulder	256 or greater	
Cobble	64-256	Conglomerate
Pebble	4-64	
Granule	2-4	

Particle	Size (millimeters)	Rock
Sand	$1/16$ - 2	Sandstone
Silt	$1/256$ - $1/16$	Siltstone
Clay	Less than $1/256$	Shale

B. CHEMICAL SEDIMENTARY ROCKS

Some sediments build up on the ocean floor when water can no longer keep various chemicals dissolved within it. Chemical sedimentary rock can be divided into two categories: those derived from organic or once-living sources and those from inorganic sources.

1. ORGANIC

Limestones

There are many different kinds of limestone, some organic and some inorganic, but all consisting of calcium carbonate, $CaCO_3$. Even those limestones which are considered to be organic in nature contain much inorganic limestone but have a significant percentage of organically derived materials such as shells of sea creatures, reef fragments, or the limey secretions of sea creatures.

Limestones are often found covering large areas. Today limey sediments are being deposited in many places, such as the Caribbean Sea. Modern limey sediments are very fine-grained sediments made primarily of aragonite, while the limestone deposits of the past were of the even finer-grained calcite. Conditions must have been different when they were deposited than conditions today.

Diatomaceous Earth

Other sedimentary deposits of interest are made up of a collection of

Illustration of a single-celled diatom (left)

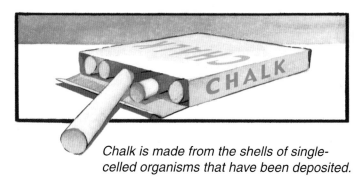

the shells from single-celled organisms called diatoms or radiolarians, and certain algae in the case of chalk. These sediments never harden into

Chalk is made from the shells of single-celled organisms that have been deposited.

very hard rock. They are used to filter and purify water for us to drink or to make chalk to write on blackboards. While these single-celled organisms do exist today, they do not collect in vast quantities as we see in the geologic record. Some other process must have been involved in their production and collection.

Coal

We have all seen the black rock called coal, which can be burned. It is used in many electrical power plants to heat water and so generate electricity. Often found in widespread layers, it is the altered remains of huge masses of buried plant material. While layers of organic material called peat

The upper and lower dark layers in this photo are two coal seams in a bluff from Prince, Utah.

Limestones

Calcium carbonate can be derived from inorganic sources as well as organic sources. Inorganic deposits are usually fairly small in lateral extent, and form today in places where the water has a great deal of mineral material dissolved in it, such as in caves or around mineral springs. Stalactites and stalagmites are formed in this way.

do accumulate today in swamps, we know of no instances where peat changes into coal under normal circumstances. Furthermore, some coal deposits cover large areas with extremely flat beds, but peat swamps are always small in comparison and quite irregular. No doubt about it — the past was different from the present.

Dolomite

A rock similar in many ways to limestone is known as dolomite, with atoms of magnesium included in the calcium carbonate. Perhaps this is accomplished by the replacement of individual atoms of calcium with magnesium, but the origin of large dolomite beds is not at all understood.

Coal is used as fuel for power in many industries (left).

Cave formations are primarily found in limestone. They were formed as groundwater evaporated, leaving its dissolved minerals behind (right).

15

Evaporites

When seawater evaporates, it leaves behind the minerals dissolved in it. Since seawater has many different minerals, including metals, dissolved in it, the evaporated remains of seawater make quite a mixture.

Sometimes, however, pure salt is found — so pure that it can be mined and put right on the kitchen table. Very few impurities or organic remains are found in it. These could not be the remains of evaporated sea water, but appear to have been formed when a huge volume of mineral-laden water came up through the ocean floor basalts and released its dissolved content when it hit the cold ocean waters. Although called evaporites, a more proper term would be precipitites. Other rock types in this category would be gypsum and anhydrite, none of which are forming today in quantities equal to those of the past.

Salt crystals (left) can often be mined directly out of the ground with very few impurities and used for table salt (above).

CHARACTERISTICS OF SEDIMENTARY ROCKS

Water is almost always in a near horizontal position when it deposits its load. Thus, the resulting beds are fairly flat. Each depositional episode of moving water will leave behind a pancake-type layer of sediments. Another pancake layer may be deposited later, on top of the first layer, separated from it by a bedding plane.

Ripple Marks and Crossbeds

Waves washing over a flat beach will leave ripple marks, but ripple marks are also found on many rock surfaces. Since nearly identical ripple marks are preserved on many bedding planes between rock layers we can discern that moving water flowed over them when the sediments were still muddy. Extremely large ripple marks are known as crossbeds and are more easily compared to huge sand dunes in an otherwise flat desert. But dry sand dunes in a desert would seldom be preserved, lacking any water to cement the grains together. On the other hand, huge underwater sand dunes can be preserved one after the other, until an entire thick deposit of crossbeds can be seen intersecting the flat-lying bedding planes.

Crossbedding can be clearly seen in the layers of Checkerboard Mesa in Utah.

Mud Cracks

When wet mud dries out it will crack into a series of polygons, and when the mud hardens, the cracks remain. In just the same way, mud can crack underground as the mud dries out, even after being buried by other sediments. As the mud hardens into stone, the cracks are preserved.

The camera lens cap shows the scale of the mud cracks above.

Concretions

Sometimes hard nodules are formed underground. These rather circular objects are thought to form around some fossil or other nucleus. Usually a nodule is harder than any rock which may surround it, and when the rock erodes, these nodules remain.

Geodes

Sometimes concretions form that are hollow and lined inside with crystals. When sliced open, these can be extremely beautiful and are used as decorations in homes.

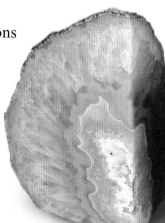

These bookends are from a section of a geode that has been cut and polished.

HOW RIPPLE MARKS ARE FORMED

Sediments under water, such as sand, settle to the bottom.

Currents in the water push the muddy sediments into ripples (above) in much the same way that the wind blows sand into dunes. The sediments later harden into sedimentary rock (below).

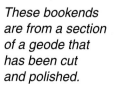

III. METAMORPHIC ROCKS

The Greek words *meta*, which means "change," and *morphe*, which means "form," are used together to mean "to change form." A caterpillar can metamorphose into a butterfly, for instance.

In just the same way, certain rocks appear to have undergone major changes and turned into some rather different sort of rock. Nothing like this is going on today on the scale of the past.

Schist

It is thought that if slate continues to undergo heat and pressure it will become a rock called schist that contains abundant mica. This rock can be split much like slate, but the plates are much more crumpled.

Slate

When shale is subjected to heat and pressure, it can be metamorphosed into slate. It readily splits into thin, even slabs and is used for roofing, blackboards, and decorative sidewalks.

Gneiss

(PRONOUNCED "NICE")

A highly metamorphosed, banded rock, gneiss is characterized by alternating bands of different minerals. These different bands are of unknown or varied origin and may be the metamorphosed remnants of sedimentary rocks or igneous rocks.

Layers of schist and marble can be seen in the photo at the left. Note the hammer for scale.

Slate is often used for blackboards in schools (right).

Quartzite

Metamorphosed quartz sandstone can turn into quartzite. It is typically extremely hard and resistant to erosion or weathering.

Marble

Evidently, when limestone metamorphoses, it changes into marble. Usually the heat and pressure destroy any remnants of fossils that were in the original rock, but in some rare cases, those fossils remain. This rock has many uses because of its beauty, especially when polished.

What Causes Metamorphism?

In general, we can say that heat and pressure are the causes of contact metamorphism of one rock into another. It happens today when a hot igneous body like granite is intruded into sedimentary rocks. The rock adjacent to the intrusion is heated and pressurized and undergoes metamorphism into a somewhat different rock.

Typically, however, metamorphic rocks are found on an incredibly large scale. Great thicknesses and areas are covered by metamorphic rock. This regional metamorphism must be due to forces more intense and conditions far different than those that are observed today.

SUMMARY OF ROCK TYPES

I. IGNEOUS ROCKS

Granite
Rhyolite
Basalt
Obsidian
Pumice

II. SEDIMENTARY ROCKS

A. CLASTIC
Shale
Sandstone
Conglomerate

B. CHEMICAL
  1. ORGANIC
Limestones
Diatomaceous earth
Coal
  2. INORGANIC
Limestones
Dolomite
Evaporites

III. METAMORPHIC ROCKS

Slate
Schist
Gneiss
Quartzite
Marble

Chapter 3

THE EARTH'S SURFACE

Now that we know what the earth is made of, we can begin to look at the shape that it is in. In this chapter we will look at the features that we can see and in the next chapter we will take a look at the processes that produce these large features.

I. PLAINS

Low-lying Plains

Since most sediments are transported by moving water, and moving water is transported by gravity, once the water reaches near sea level it no longer has much force. Here it begins to deposit its sediment load in flat-lying plains, typically a few hundred feet above or below sea level.

This photo of the Baton Rouge, Louisiana area (left) was taken from Skylab 3 in earth's orbit. The alluvial plains of the Mississippi River can be seen down the middle of the photo. Because of the rich sediments, plains make up some of the richest farmland in America (below).

Alluvial Plains

Rivers, such as the Mississippi River, carry great amounts of sediment in their waters. Sediments called alluvial sediments will be deposited whenever the water slows down, such as when it goes around a bend or as it enters the ocean, forming a delta. In a delta, these sediments can cover quite a large area.

Coastal Plains

Many such plains are found upriver or uphill from an alluvial plain. These may have been uplifted with little or no bending. Perhaps sea level has dropped since deposition.

Lake Plains

Lake waters contain sediments too, and these can be deposited in a lake bed. Perhaps at a later

HOW LAKE PLAINS ARE FORMED

A lake will deposit layers of sediment along the bottom of the lake forming large flat areas.

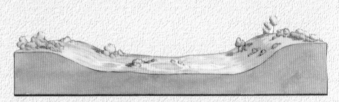

As the lake dries up it will deposit the rest of its sediments and vegetation will begin to grow.

The sediments will eventually dry completely forming the solid ground of a plain.

time the lake will evaporate or will be uplifted and these lake plains, sometimes known as lacustrine plains, will be exposed.

Death Valley (left) is a lake plain that was formed as the water dried up, leaving its sediments behind. The mountains in the distance held the lake water. Run-off sediments can be seen at the foot of the mountain.

Glacial Plains

Sometimes glaciers level the ground beneath into a flat plain. The ice, however, contains sediments, and as the ice melts these sediments will be deposited on the flat, eroded surface.

Lava Plains

When lava from a volcano solidifies, it becomes like a sedimentary rock as well. Since the lava was a liquid, the lava tends to stay in a fairly level pool, which then hardens into a lava plain.

Offshore Deposits

Sediments entering the ocean by rivers or streams will form a delta if the ocean currents are low. If stronger currents are present the sediments will be distributed offshore in a broad plain. Sedimentation is enhanced in calm waters, such as between the coast and an offshore island, or in the deep ocean.

This topographical map shows the locations of the plains, plateaus, and mountains in North America. Plains are shown in green, plateaus in yellow, mountains in brown.

II. PLATEAUS

Plateaus are also essentially flat-lying sediment layers. They are underlain either by horizontal rock strata or a rather horizontal erosional surface. Their distinguishing feature, however, is that they are at higher elevations. For instance, the Colorado Plateau, which covers several states in the western United States, is at an average elevation of about 5,000 feet. The rock materials themselves were formed underwater, but they are no longer receiving sediments. Instead, they are eroding.

How Plateaus are Formed

When rock breaks and a large flat area is uplifted then a fault plateau is formed.

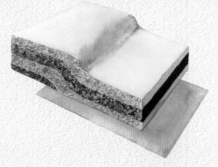

A warped plateau is caused by a slow uplifting of rock that doesn't break.

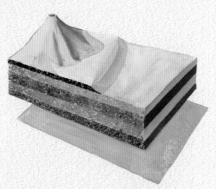

A lava plateau is formed by flat layers of hardened lava.

Fault Plateaus

One way a plateau can be uplifted is through faults, where the rock beneath is broken and shoved up. The Colorado Plateau in the western United States was formed in this way as ocean bottom rocks were uplifted over a mile in elevation.

Warped Plateaus

Due to regional squeezing or slow uplift, some rock units are uplifted without major faulting. These are typically crumpled and warped. The Appalachian Mountains in the eastern United States have many

areas that are quite crumpled and other areas that are flat. They would fit into this category of a warped plateau.

Lava Plateaus

Sometimes huge plateaus of basalt are found at higher elevations. They may have been formed as pools of lava hardened at these elevations, or perhaps have been uplifted. The Columbia River basalts in Washington and Oregon are an example of this kind of lava plateau.

Plateaus are similar to plains but are at higher elevations (left and below).

Every mountain looks different. Some are sharp, some are rounded, some covered with trees, and some are barren. All are beautiful, making them favorite places for hiking and camping. Despite their differences, they can be grouped into one of several different categories.

The Rocky Mountains (above) were formed as layers of rock were folded and buckled under pressure. Mount Ararat (below) was formed by a series of volcanic eruptions. Today, it is 17,000 feet (5,182 m) high. The Bible states that Noah's ark landed on the mountains of Ararat.

Folded Mountains

Imagine a wooden box with several different layers of colored clay covering its bottom. Now imagine that you bring two of the sides closer together crumpling the clay in between. In some places the clay would be pushed up into "mountains" and in between would be valleys. In just that way, some mountains of sediments have been crumpled up by pressures from the side. The Alps, the Himalayas, the Appalachians, and the Rocky Mountains are all due in part to such forces from the side. Even though some places in these mountains are still flat, overall there is much evidence of folding.

Domed Mountains

If we were to take the same layers of flat-lying clay and push on them from the bottom they would dome up into a mountain, with the stratified sediments sloping down on each side. The Black Hills of South Dakota are this type of mountain.

Fault Block Mountains

Now imagine that we cut the flat-lying sediments vertically with a knife and push up only one side. The side that would be higher would be like a mountain compared to the valley on the other side. The Grand Teton Mountains in

Wyoming are in this category. Some mountain chains are much more complicated than can be described by these simple experiments. These would perhaps be called combination or complex mountains. The Adirondack Mountains of New York and the White Mountains of New Hampshire would fall into these complex types of mountains.

Volcanic Mountains

When molten lavas from deep inside the earth's crust are pushed out onto the surface, they form volcanic mountains. Many times volcanoes lie in linear chains. The volcanic islands of Hawaii are an example of this kind of mountain. Many volcanic mountains can be seen in the Pacific Northwest, including Mount Rainier and Mount St. Helens.

The Bible says that Noah's ark came to rest on "the mountains of Ararat" (Gen. 8:4). The mountain which today goes by the name Mount Ararat is a volcanic mountain 17,000 feet (5,182 m) high. It gives evidence of having erupted many times during the flood and also after the flood.

HOW MOUNTAINS ARE FORMED

Folded

An easy way to understand how mountains are formed is to compare it to working with layers of clay. If you squeeze the sides of the clay together then the layers will buckle and fold. This is how folded mountains are formed. Layers of rock are buckled and folded up into mountains because of forces pressing in on them.

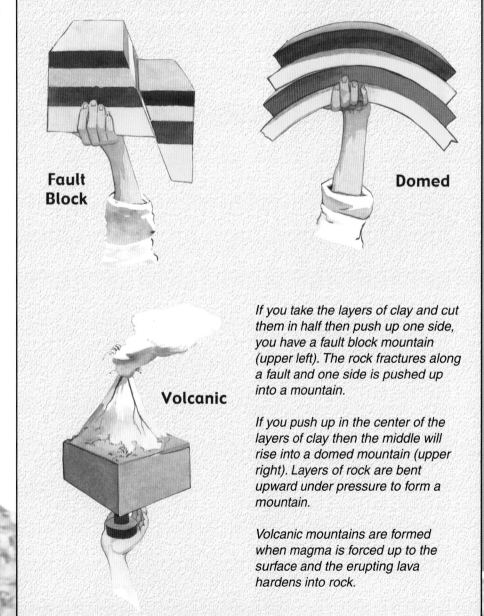

Fault Block

Domed

Volcanic

If you take the layers of clay and cut them in half then push up one side, you have a fault block mountain (upper left). The rock fractures along a fault and one side is pushed up into a mountain.

If you push up in the center of the layers of clay then the middle will rise into a domed mountain (upper right). Layers of rock are bent upward under pressure to form a mountain.

Volcanic mountains are formed when magma is forced up to the surface and the erupting lava hardens into rock.

IV. Erosional Features

Some of the most dramatic geologic features on planet Earth are actually due to erosion rather than mountain-building.

Canyons

Streams and rivers can carve deep canyons like the Grand Canyon. Exposed on the sides of these canyons may be the flat-lying sediments. Canyons are sometimes the favorite places for geologists to study because the rocks are exposed so well. They can "read" these rocks like pages in a book.

The Grand Canyon was formed by water eroding the canyon.

Continental Shields

The predominantly granite core of the continents is seldom exposed. Usually it is covered by sedimentary rock, but a glacier flowing over a continent might scrape off all of the sedimentary rock and expose the granite once the ice melts. Once both the sedimentary rock and the ice are gone, the granite tends to bulge up because there is no more weight on top of it. Manhattan Island is an example of scraped-off and exposed granite.

Much of the interior of Canada is like this, with the huge predominantly granite core covered only by minor amounts of soil and rock.

Areas such as Manhattan Island were caused by a glacier scraping off the sedimentary rock down to the granite core.

Remnants of Erosion

Sometimes when water flows over an area of flat-lying strata, much erosion will take place, but once the water is gone, isolated high places will remain. These are not true mountains but are sometimes called mountains because they are higher than the surrounding area.

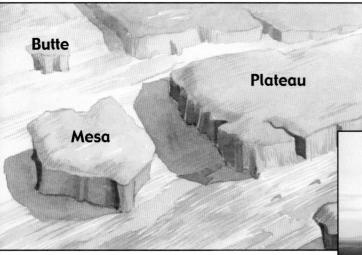

Butte

Plateau

Mesa

Much of the western United States shows evidence of water erosion on a major scale. Buttes (below) and "hoodoos" (bottom of page) are areas that were left standing while the ground around them was eroded away.

One such feature is called a mesa, which is a broad, flat-topped hill rising above the surrounding lowlands.

A butte has a smaller, narrower top than a mesa, with steep-sided edges.

These features are frequently seen in the western United States where the terrain is not covered by much vegetation and the geologic features are easily seen. They exist in the eastern United States also, such as in the Catskill Mountains of eastern New York and the Allegheny Mountains in West Virginia and Lookout Mountain in Tennessee.

The volcanic ash spewed out by a volcano is easily eroded. Once it is gone, it leaves behind a volcanic plug or neck, which is the central tube of lava that cooled inside the mountain. Devil's Tower in Wyoming has such a history.

Sometimes old mountain ranges are almost completely eroded with only a few remnants still standing. These are called monadnocks, named after Mount Monadnock in New Hampshire. Stone Mountain in Georgia is another example of this.

Next time you fly over the states of Arizona, Utah, and Nevada, look out of the window of the airplane and see if you can imagine what sort of an erosional event would have caused the features that you see.

Notice that many of the features look like the much smaller features that you might see in a sloping muddy field after a big rain. Once the rain was over and the water had drained off, you would see a number of "canyons." Some areas would be quite eroded with a few mesas or buttes sticking up. This eroded material may have been deposited at the base of the hill in a plain.

Now, in your mind, multiply that rainfall by many thousands of times and think about the flood of Noah's day. What would have been the result of those waters as they rushed back into the ocean at the end of the flood? Could the eroded terrain that you see in Arizona and Utah be the result of that massive event?

Chapter 4

GEOLOGICAL PROCESSES AND RATES

Now that we have some understanding of the nature of the earth around us, let's talk about the processes which may have formed it and which continue to shape it.

I. EROSION

Everything in the universe is subject to the law of disintegration. If processes continue as they do today, eventually everything will be eroded and worn away. Sometimes the process is slow, sometimes fast, and so it is even with rock. If exposed to the elements of nature, it is eroding away. Physical processes such as freezing and thawing can speed up this process of disintegration, as ice expands and exerts pressure on the surrounding rock. In many cases this is enough to break down the rock.

When sunlight heats the rock, it might expand and little pieces can break away.

Rocks can also be broken down by the activities of plants and animals. The roots of plants can break rock as can the burrowing of rodents, worms, and insects.

PROCESSES OF NORMAL EROSION

Water is one of the driving forces of erosion. Even **rain** over time can erode mountains.

Water seeps down into the cracks in rocks. When the water **freezes** it expands, and when it **thaws**, it contracts, breaking the rocks.

rainwater can move many particles and dissolve other chemicals. The more grit, pebbles, and rocks being carried away by the water, the more damage they will do to the underlying rock. Obviously, the greater amount and velocity of the moving water, the greater the damage to the rock over which it flows.

Erosion shapes nearly every feature of the world around us. Canyons (above) are formed by water dissolving away one kind of rock while leaving the rocks around it. A natural bridge (right) is formed in much the same way with the rock under the bridge having eroded away.

Another type of decomposition is known as chemical weathering. The presence of oxygen in the air causes some of the rock minerals to change. Other minerals absorb water and change their chemical structure. Sometimes chemicals in the rocks may be dissolved by the water.

All of these processes occur on a daily basis, but one will normally never notice the effects unless the processes have gone on for years. However, when processes are unusually rapid and dynamic, great amounts of geologic work can be accomplished.

For instance, the pounding of raindrops in a heavy rain can cause damage. The drainage of

Erosion by Hurricanes

We think of hurricanes as storms with high winds and great rainfall. But actually, flooding done by hurricanes often causes the greatest damage — at times the damage is incredible. Beaches have been removed. The foundations of buildings have been undercut and the buildings have fallen. Huge canyons have appeared from nowhere.

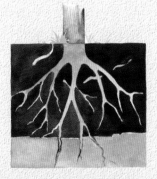

Plants and **animals** cause erosion by worms burrowing holes through soil and tree roots breaking rock as they grow.

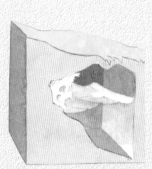

Chemical erosion takes place when chemicals in the air and water react with minerals in rocks, dissolving them.

Ocean waves constantly pound the shores, eroding the rocks and soil.

Berlingame Canyon

In the state of Washington the government maintained a series of ditches to provide irrigation for the farmers and ranchers of the area. In 1926 a major storm caused the ditches to fill to overflowing. Eventually one ditch was clogged. The water in the ditch was temporarily diverted, so that the ditch could be cleaned out, but suddenly the water from the ditch began eroding a gulch, and within a short period of time a canyon 150 feet (46 m) deep was eroded in the adjacent hillside.

Glen Canyon Dam

Part of the Colorado River system, Lake Powell in Arizona backs up behind Glen Canyon Dam. In June of 1983 the melting of excessive winter snow in the Rocky Mountains caused the lake to fill to dangerously high levels. Fearing damage to the dam, engineers opened a 40-foot (12 m) diameter drainage tunnel to remove some of the water. They gradually increased the quantity and velocity of water until suddenly the strength of the concrete and steel tunnel was exceeded, and

When a hurricane, such as the one seen in the satellite image above, hits the shore with its wind, rain, and flooding, it generates massive amounts of erosion.

huge chunks of concrete broke off and were hurled from the tunnel. The water turned red, the color of the surrounding rock.

As quickly as possible the tunnel was closed, but in just a very short period of time (probably not much more than a minute) a huge hole 32 feet (10 m) deep, 150 feet (46 m) long, and 40 feet (12 m) wide had been cut through the 3-foot (1 m) thick concrete and into the red sandstone bedrock. Rapidly moving water has incredible erosive power.

Berlingame Canyon was eroded in less than two days when an irrigation ditch overflowed. This "Little Grand Canyon" shows how the Grand Canyon itself could have been eroded by rapidly moving water.

Rapid Erosive Processes

When water is flowing faster than 20 miles per hour, tiny vacuum bubbles are formed along the surface. These bubbles explode inwardly and pound the rock with great force, reducing it to powder in a process called cavitation.

A second erosion process is called plucking. When high velocity water flows over a rock, it sometimes is able to rip up loose blocks of bedrock and move them along the bottom. Not only is the chunk of rock removed in this process, but it pulverizes the rock on which it bounces.

A third energetic process is due to an underwater tornado called a kolk. Just like a tornado in the air, it can lift and remove large chunks of the underlying material.

Thus, we see while normal weathering, rainfall, solar heating, tidal action, freezing, thawing, etc., can do a sure and steady work, the action of major high-energy events is far, far greater.

This hole at the base of the tunnel (right) was eroded in probably not much more than a minute when engineers at Glen Canyon Dam tried to relieve water pressure to the dam by using the drainage tunnel.

RAPID EROSION

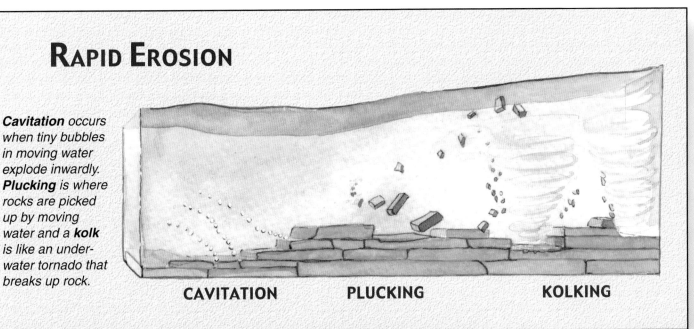

Cavitation *occurs when tiny bubbles in moving water explode inwardly.* **Plucking** *is where rocks are picked up by moving water and a* **kolk** *is like an underwater tornado that breaks up rock.*

CAVITATION   **PLUCKING**   **KOLKING**

31

II. DEPOSITION

Sedimentary deposits can occur through the action of water, wind, and ice. Wind-blown deposits rarely result in sedimentation that hardens into rock, and the work of glaciers is confined to the polar ice caps and high mountains. Thus, nearly all the sedimentation which lasts is done through the action of water in combination with the force of gravity.

The speed with which the water flows primarily depends on how sloped the surface is. If the surface is quite steep the water travels rapidly, and where the ground is flat the water slows

Many of the sediments in lakes come from the rivers picking up dirt and pebbles in the mountains and then depositing them when they enter the lake.

down and almost stops. As a general rule, where the water is flowing rapidly it will erode the rock over which it is passing, and when it slows down it deposits whatever sediments it contains.

Lakes

Consider a river flowing through a mountain, picking up dirt and pebbles and sand grains along the way. As the river enters the lake, the water slows down and all the particles contained in the water settle to the bottom of the lake. Thus, the bottom of the lake is quite muddy.

Deltas

A major river like the Mississippi River contains a great deal of sediment eroded from rainfall and other activity upstream. Perhaps you have seen the Mississippi River and noticed how muddy the water looks. As the river reaches the coastal plain of Louisiana, it spreads out into a delta looking much like a bird's foot, dividing into numerous smaller rivers.

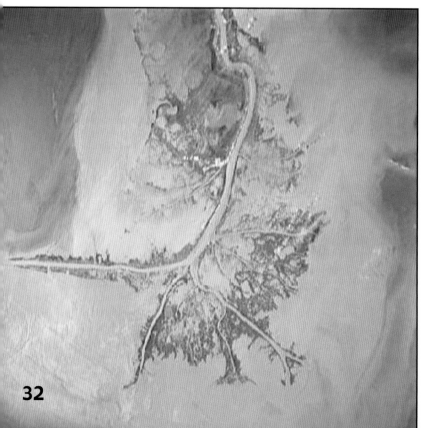

A satellite image of the Mississippi River Delta where it turns into a "bird's foot." The main river divides up into smaller and smaller rivers and streams where the water slows down to enter the Gulf of Mexico. As the water slows, it deposits much of its sediment load.

As the waters enter the Gulf of Mexico, they slow down and all the sediments begin to drop out on the sea floor. As these muds gather underwater, the bottom of the Gulf in that area is filled until it nears the water's surface. So, the water takes the sediments out farther and farther. In this way, the delta deposits grow farther and farther out to sea.

Offshore Deposition

Any place the waters have high energy they will erode the rock surface. As the waves crash into the shoreline, great erosion sometimes takes place. This not only provides sand for the beach, but as the waves go back into the ocean, they often deposit material in an offshore bar or offshore island as their energy is lost.

Rivers

Some rivers, as they meander along in an "S" fashion, will tend to erode the bank on the outside of the "S" curve and deposit sediment on the inside where the energy is less.

On a day-to-day basis with normal energy levels, the erosion and deposition tend to be in equilibrium and not much geologic work is done. However, on rare high-energy occasions, geologic work can occur quite rapidly.

Turbidites

In 1927 a major event happened off the Canadian coast of Newfoundland through which geologists learned much about rapid deposition. Without warning, an earthquake occurred which caused a great volume of loose sediments on the continental shelf to slide as an underwater avalanche. The mud raced down the slope at 60 miles per hour and eventually came to rest on the ocean bottom. This underwater mud flow behaved much as wet cement

An "S" shaped river erodes the outside of the curve and deposits its sediments on the inside.

HOW A TURBIDITE IS FORMED

First, an event such as an earthquake starts a mud flow underwater.

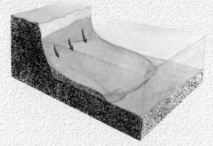

Next, the mud flow spreads out, much like wet cement.

Eventually, the mud flow hardens into a layer of rock.

behaves flowing off a cement truck. When it finally lost its energy and came to a halt, it had covered an area of 40,000 square miles (12,192 m²) with a deposit two to three feet (0.6-1 m) thick.

In the 1950s and 1960s geologists were able to study this deposit with the help of submarines. Through this study they were able to define a "turbidite" as the result of catastrophic water

The Tapeats Sandstone can be seen in the Grand Canyon as a dark flat layer. Scientists believe that it was formed by a series of underwater flows of sand.

currents. To their surprise, they realized that turbidites are similar in character to many solidified rocks that had already been studied in the Appalachian Mountains and the Rocky Mountains, which geologists thought had been deposited by calm

waters. They now recognize that many, if not most of the rocks on land are actually turbidites, too.

Other catastrophic deposits are now recognized mainly by observing the activity of hurricanes. They sometimes deposit great volumes of sand and rock on the beach. This material is usually eroded fairly quickly in the weeks that follow as the tides and waves do their normal work.

These modern-day geologic and watery catastrophes help us understand what the flood of Noah's day must have been like.

Deposition on a Grand Scale

During great floods, energy levels are much higher than anything we normally experience and they operate over wide areas. Take a look at one major sedimentary rock called the Tapeats Sandstone, which can be seen in the lower part of the Grand Canyon. It is a very hard rock, resistant to erosion, and forms a distinct brown cliff.

In previous years, geologists pointed to the variety of internal layers within this 100 to 325-foot-thick (30-100 m) sedimentary

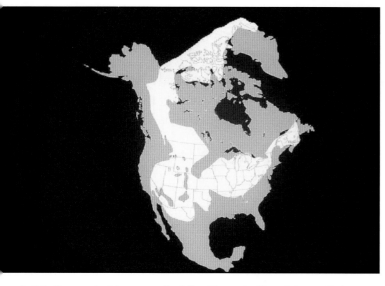

A thin "pancake" layer, called the Tapeats Sandstone (light yellow), covers most of North America. It would have taken a great underwater event to create such a formation.

locations show that the Tapeats Sandstone exists (with various names) as a pancake-like layer covering most of the North American continent.

At the base of the Tapeats Sandstone is an incredibly flat erosional surface, from which all of the previous materials had been eroded, leaving a flat surface on which the Tapeats "pancake" could be deposited.

Tidal Waves (Tsunamis)

Sometimes when an underwater earthquake or volcanic eruption occurs, a shock wave of energy races through the water. In the deep ocean this shock wave does little damage, but once it nears a continent it becomes a wall

rock and thought that this kind of layering was due to slow and gradual deposition on the bottom of a calm ocean. Now that more is known, however, geologists have concluded that the Tapeats Sandstone was due to a series of underwater flows of sand racing along at speeds of up to 90 miles per hour (145 km/h). Such devastating sand flows comprised a highly energetic event and must have been caused by an even greater event.

This same sandstone, with its distinctive character and content, can be seen in many places around the United States. Even when it is not exposed on the surface, it can be observed as oil well drillers bore through it. A map of these

Tsunamis are giant tidal waves that pick up sediments and slam them into the shore (above). The damage from the wall of water and the flooding can be enormous (left).

of water which slams into the shoreline. At first it picks up anything in its path, and then deposits the load of sediments, clams, and other sea creatures which it has carried along.

What kind of event would be able to maintain such high energy levels all across the continents? Only the flood of Noah's day fits those requirements.

Contrary to common belief, it does not take a long time for sediments to harden into sedimentary rock. It just takes the right conditions.

It does not take a long time for sedimentary rock to form. There are many examples where rock has formed on objects left in sea water, such as the set of keys above.

Modern Examples

There are many examples where sedimentary rocks will form around a metal object left in seawater. A bobby pin lost in the sand or a ship's bell from a sunken ship is often discovered with a crust of rock surrounding it. This happens when the seawater dissolves some of the iron minerals in the metal object. The iron then becomes the basis for a cement or glue which binds the sand grains together into a hard rock. In a very similar way, sediments can harden fairly rapidly into sedimentary rock. It does not take a long time; it just takes the right conditions.

Compaction

Have you ever noticed that when you have a bucket full of sand, so full that you cannot get any more sand into it, that you can still pour a great deal of water into the bucket. The water comes to rest in the openings between the sand grains. Loose sand is actually about 50 percent open space in which water can be trapped (or oil, or natural gas).

Obviously, sand can harden into sandstone, but in doing so it must be compacted. In a typical sandstone usually only 10 to 20 percent of the total volume is made up of open space.

When a pancake layer of sediments is covered with other pancakes, the sand grains are pushed closer together, squeezing the water out. Compaction is the first step in turning sediment into a sedimentary rock, but not the only necessary step.

This 100-foot cliff of sedimentary rock was formed at Mount St. Helens by deposits less than five years old (left).

Sedimentary rocks are often characterized by extensive flat layers (right).

Cementation

The next step involves the addition of some sort of glue, which will bind the grains together into a hard, solid rock. Sand is made up primarily of the mineral silica, and when hot water encounters the silica, some of it is dissolved. Once the water cools off and stops migrating, then that silica can be redeposited and glues the sand grains together.

In limestones, a primary mineral is calcite, which likewise can be dissolved and transported by warm waters, which then can solidify the entire rock.

Once these right conditions are met, the sediments can harden quite quickly into sedimentary rock.

When Mount St. Helens erupted in 1980, its melted glacier avalanched down its slopes. It left behind, in places, a stack of pancake-like layers of sediments up to 600-feet-thick (183 m) made up of sand-grain-sized particles, which contained a great deal of silica.

Obviously, the "pancake" sediments were quite warm, and soon water had dissolved enough of the silica to bind this sandy deposit into a fairly hard sandstone. In five years, eroded sections were able to stand as near-vertical cliffs. Loose sand cannot stand in such a cliff, but hard rock can. It doesn't take long to harden sediments into sedimentary rock, if the conditions are met.

HOW SEDIMENTARY ROCKS ARE FORMED

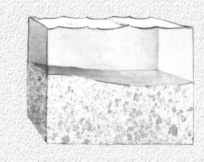

*First, layers of sediment are deposited. The weight of the water and the sediments on top begin to **compact** the sediments underneath.*

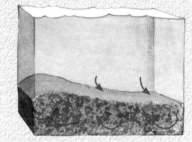

*Next, warm water circulates throughout the sediments and **dissolves** certain minerals. The dissolved minerals surround the individual grains of sediment.*

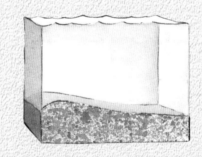

*Finally, when the water cools off and stops moving, the dissolved minerals act as a "glue" that **cements** the grains of sediment together to form sedimentary rock.*

IV. FOSSILIZATION

Fossils are the remains of plants and animals that were once alive. But how can something that is dead be preserved for a long time? Think about your own experience. All animals eventually die. When a rat dies in the woods, or a buffalo dies on the prairie, or a fish dies in the ocean, what happens to its body? Scavengers, other animals or insects will eat the body or perhaps tiny bacteria will cause it to decompose. Maybe the oxygen or other chemicals in the air will cause it to totally deteriorate. Once-living material seldom lasts very long under normal circumstances after it dies.

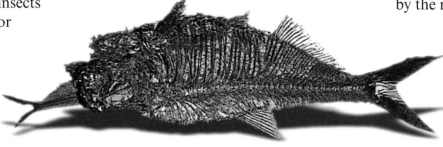

There are many examples that show fossils form rapidly, such as this fish that was fossilized in the process of swallowing another fish.

Yet we have billions and trillions of fossils. Fish and other marine creatures are often fossilized in tremendous numbers, some of them in the process of giving birth, others in the process of eating another. It is almost like a snapshot of their life. How did this happen?

In places, thousands of dinosaur bones are buried and fossilized, comprising entire hillsides.

The great majority of fossils are creatures with hard parts, like clams or coral, which lived on the ocean bottom. These are preserved by the multiplied trillions.

Under normal circumstances today, no fossils are being formed. What happened in the past to cause them to be preserved in such large numbers? There are many different conditions under which it could happen, but the main requirement is that the organism be buried rapidly. It must be protected from scavengers which will eat it and it must be where bacteria and chemicals cannot decompose it. Once it is protected, then the agents of fossilization can take over and turn it into a fossil.

A fossil ammonite (left)

A T-rex skull (right)

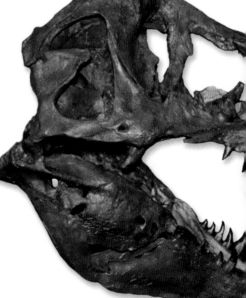

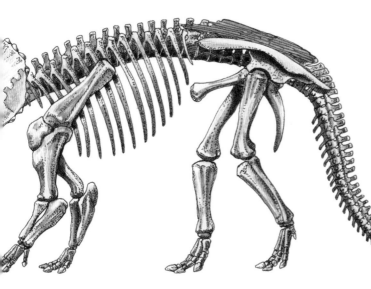

The Different Types of Fossils

1. Only Hard Parts Are Preserved

Because hard parts of an organism are the most resistant to decay and least likely to be eaten, this type of fossil is extremely common. Among land animals it is most common to find the teeth, bones, or tusks. For marine animals, the hard shells are quite common, as is coral. Often, the bony or shelly material is still present. Sometimes you can see the pearly sheen of the oyster shell. Bones may still have the cell structure visible.

A mammoth tooth

Often these types of bones are found in huge graveyards with animals from many different environments buried together.

2. Replacement by Other Materials

Frequently, after the organism has been deposited, it will decay underground and its molecules will be carried away by water moving through the rock. But the water will have other dissolved materials in it and may replace the organism with the other material.

This material is usually the same material that is in the rock, but because of its different time of sedimentation, it retains the shape of the creature.

3. A Cast or Mold Is All that Remains

Sometimes the organic material decays, but the rocks surrounding it have already solidified. This will leave an open space in the place of the organism. It may later be filled with something else.

A very famous cast was that of a hippopotamus caught in a lava flow. The body of the hippo was totally covered. Later when the body decayed, it left a cave the size and shape of a hippo.

4. Petrification

Wood can be petrified when it is buried in an area where hot silica-rich waters flow. The water seeps around every cell in the wood encasing it in silica, or in some cases removing the organic material and replacing it with silica. Many times the preservation is so precise you can still count the tree rings.

In Yellowstone Park, trees are living in areas frequently covered by hot silica-rich waters. Even while the tree is still alive, petrification of its roots and lower trunk begins.

There are cases where animals or even human bodies have been petrified. They were buried in an area where hot silica-rich waters migrate through.

Trees can be turned into stone when they are buried in an area with silica-rich water.

Dinosaur fossil before it has been cut out of the rock.

years, that amber hardens, preserving the insect inside. Even some DNA fragments are preserved. The thought that a dinosaur might be reconstructed from the DNA in its blood after having been bitten by a mosquito preserved in amber is totally fictional. DNA simply does not last that long once the organism is dead.

7. FROZEN ANIMALS

In Siberia and Alaska many millions of mammoth bones have been preserved. These animals lived during the Ice Age following Noah's flood. On occasion one would get frozen in unusual conditions and even the flesh and hair were preserved, but these fossils are extremely rare.

5. CARBONIZATION

All living things are made up of carbon, hydrogen, and water. Under some circumstances, the water and hydrogen can be removed leaving just the carbon. We know that coal is the remains of plant materials, because on many occasions the impressions of the plants are still present. Oil seems to be the remains of marine algae having undergone a similar burial and carbonization.

The Limestone Cowboy. From the boot we can tell that this cowboy died sometime after 1950. But his body was in a petrified state when discovered in 1980.

8. ANIMAL TRACKS AND WORM BURROWS

Fossilized worm burrows are fairly common in the geologic strata. Once the sediments were deposited, the then-still-living worms or clams or other organisms tried to burrow out. Almost all burrows show that the animals were burrowing toward the upper surface. They did not appreciate being buried alive, but many were buried too deep to get out.

On occasion we find animal tracks. Dinosaur tracks are the most famous. One very famous study of fossilized lizard or amphibian tracks in the Grand Canyon helped show that a particular sandstone bed was not a desert sand dune deposit as some thought, but a rippled underwater sand

6. THE PRESERVATION OF SOFT PARTS

This type of fossilization is quite rare, but somewhat famous. Sometimes an insect will be entombed in amber and over the

Trilobite fossils (left)

Fossilized dinosaur tracks (right)

flow deposit. How could an amphibian make tracks which would remain in dry desert sand? It would have to be in wet sand.

9. COPROLITES

It is hard to imagine, but there have been some fossilized examples of dung found in the rocks. The dung can be examined under a microscope and is found to contain remains of the organism's last meal.

10. GASTROLITHS

Today some birds eat tiny pebbles or sand grains to help them digest their food. In much the same way,

Clam Fossils

dinosaurs or other large reptiles must have done this in the past, because on occasion a dinosaur fossil is found with many smoothly polished stones inside its body.

HOW DINOSAUR FOSSILS ARE FORMED

First, if a dinosaur was not on the ark, then it drowned in the flood.

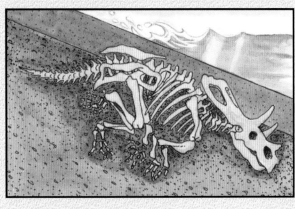

Next, the animal was buried rapidly as the flood deposited soft layers of material that later hardened into stone.

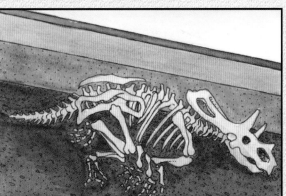

Then, a process of fossilization occurred, such as the bones being replaced by dissolved minerals in the ground water.

Finally, the fossils became exposed as the ground around the animal eroded away.

Volcanoes used to be filled with mystery, but in recent years we have learned a great deal about them.

In 1943, a farmer in Mexico was out working in his fields when he noticed steam coming up from the ground. Then he noticed several small rocks being thrown into the air, and before long there was a pile of rocks, and then a hill of rocks. Within one week the hill was 350 feet (107 m) high and by the end of the first year it was 1,400 feet (427 m) high. The mountain ceased activity in about nine years, but we learned a lot from it.

Mount St. Helens erupted in a cloud of ash and debris (left). Later, hot lava pushed its way to the surface forming a lava dome (right).

Mount St. Helens

On May 18, 1980, Mount St. Helens in southern Washington erupted. Geologists had observed this mountain carefully for years and knew that it was to erupt soon. By knowing exactly what happened at Mount St. Helens, we are able to understand what may have happened in volcanic eruptions of the past.

Some volcanoes erupt by just spilling lava out from their top. In some cases, however, the lava down inside the earth has much gas and water mixed in with it, which expands rapidly and explodes out the top. At Mount St. Helens it exploded through its side, causing great damage to everything in the area.

St. Helens Eruption

While the explosion and the ash that fell from the sky were devastating, most of the damage was done by mud flows, particularly as the glacier up near the summit melted and rapidly avalanched down the side of the volcano. One mud flow after another

Lava, steam, and ash erupt out of the opening at the top called a CRATER

SIDE VENT

Lava sometimes collects in a SILL where it does not find an outlet to the surface. It cools and becomes solid rock between layers.

Mount Ararat

One favorite mountain of those who believe the Bible is Mount Ararat in eastern Turkey. The Bible says that Noah's ark came to rest on the mountains of Ararat at the end of the flood.

This mountain is a volcanic mountain, and its most recent eruption was in 1840. Observers reported a sideward directed blast and numerous mud flows, much like those at Mount St. Helens.

It may be that the volcanic ash from an eruption of Mount Ararat after the flood is what has preserved the ark. Many eyewitnesses have said that the ark appears to be petrified. It would be petrified if it were trapped in volcanic ash.

Many believe that Noah's ark is in Ahora Gorge on Mount Ararat (above). Ash from eruptions may have preserved the ark by petrifying the wood.

deposited "pancake" layers of sediments at the base of the mountain covering many square miles in area. In that first afternoon, a great thickness of water-deposited strata had been laid down. Geologists had formerly thought that it would take long periods of time to deposit such thicknesses of sediments, but here they observed them to form in just one afternoon.

Trapped inside this material were many trees, which are now petrifying, being injected with the hot silica-rich waters flowing through these volcanic deposits.

Volcanoes of Long Ago

Recent volcanoes, as destructive as they are, are not even comparable to volcanoes of the past. For instance, the eruption which produced Yellowstone National Park was tens of thousands of times more energetic than any we have witnessed in recent years.

Lava fountain of the Pu`u `O`o cinder and spatter cone in Hawaii.

It does not appear that the Yellowstone volcano is in any danger of erupting, but there is still a great deal of heat underground as evidenced by the multitude of hot springs, smoking fumaroles, bubbling mud pots, and erupting geysers.

The **CONE** is made up of layers of hardened lava and ash.

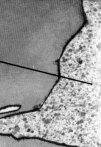

MAIN VENT

When molten magma pushes its way up from below, it collects in **MAGMA CHAMBERS**. When the pressure builds up from the heat of the mantle, the magma is forced up to the surface through vents causing a volcanic eruption.

43

Sedimentary rocks are usually laid down in a flat position, but as we know, they may have been buckled and broken by events since that time. Rocks which are already hard can be broken. They are brittle, and when subjected to outside forces they can and do fracture. When little or no movement occurs after the fracture, it is called a joint; but when there is movement, it is called a fault.

After a solid substance breaks along a diagonal plane, one side will be above the other. The higher

Sometimes rock bends instead of breaking under force. If the rock buckles up then it is an anticline. (left), but if it buckles down then it is a syncline.

side is called the hanging wall of the fault and the lower one is called the foot wall. In a fault, one of these walls will move more, or in a direction different than the other. If the hanging wall moves down, it is called a normal fault. If the hanging wall moves up it is called a reverse fault. If neither one moves up or down, but they move sideways, it is called a strike-slip fault.

MOVEMENT ALONG A FAULT

*Before major movement occurs along a fault, everything may appear normal on the surface even though there is a fracture underground. After faulting, one side of the fault will be above the other. The side which is above the fault plane is called the **hanging wall**; and the side below the fault plane is called the **foot wall** (right).*

*When forces build up to the breaking point, the sections move in one of three ways. In a **normal fault**, the hanging wall moves downward relative to the **foot wall** (below).*

This normal fault occurred near Hebgen Lake, Montana, after the magnitude 7.1 earthquake of August 18, 1959.

Folding

Instead of fracturing, the rocks may bend in response to the applied force. If the layers have buckled up, it is called an anticline, if they have buckled down it is called a syncline. If there is only one dipping zone connecting two flat zones, it is called a monocline.

Earthquakes

Movements in the earth's crust, such as bending or breaking, would be accompanied by earthquakes. When these earthquakes occur on land, they can devastate an area. If they occur in the ocean, they might produce a tsunami or tidal wave, which would devastate the coastline.

The bending or breaking of the earth's crust can result in devastating earthquakes (right).

*In a **reverse fault** (above), the hanging wall moves upward.*

*In a **strike-slip** fault (right), both walls move sideways.*

An example of a large strike-slip fault can be seen in this aerial view of the San Andreas fault in California (far right).

Bending or Breaking: Which?

An 8.5 magnitude earthquake in Anchorage, Alaska, caused the ground to shift, breaking this school building in half.

Sometimes rocks will bend instead of break as in this section of the Tapeats Sandstone. Note the people for scale (below).

Will an individual rock bend or break when subjected to outside forces? Many factors are involved, but obviously if the rock is soft, it might tend to bend; if it is very brittle it would tend to break.

Even hard rocks, however, if deeply buried, might bend instead of break, but there is usually some evidence of this when you study the rock under a microscope.

On some occasions the rocks are very tightly folded, with no evidence, even under the microscope, that they were ever hard. Since, if the conditions are right, it does not take long for sediments to harden into sedimentary rock, we can conclude that some of these tightly folded rocks were actually in a soft, unhardened condition when they folded. Usually, geologists claim that rocks had already existed for long periods of time before bending, but tight folds show this to be wrong. A better idea is needed, such as that given in Scripture. Rocks which were laid down early in the year of the great flood may have been deformed later in that year when they were still soft.

Without question, the earth's crust is divided into numerous geologic regions called plates, with boundaries identified by areas of earthquake activity. Some minor movement between these plates has been detected, but the question remains: Were the continents once connected? Did they separate some time in the past? Surprising as it may seem to students who think this has been proved, scientists have noted many unsolved problems.

Evidence for Continental Separation

It is easy to see that the continents seem to fit together. The obvious fit of Africa and South America can hardly be denied. Several arrangements of a past super continent have been proposed, with only minor amounts of overlap or gap between them.

Perhaps even more impressive is the matching of the rock layers on opposite sides of a proposed split. Even disjointed mountain chains and fault systems seem to span the ocean.

Furthermore, comparing the apparent time of formation of the continents versus the time of formation of the oceanic crust, it appears that the oceanic crust is younger, evidently having formed as the continents split apart.

There is evidence that the continents were once connected into one large super continent called Pangea (above). It would have taken a global event to have moved the continents to their current location today (right). The edges of plates are indicated by yellow lines.

Problems

The idea that the continents were once together and separated at some time in the unobserved past is far from settled. The most important problem is that there is no apparent way to move the continents. The continents are too big to push; they would crumble. They are too big to pull, they would break. The continental plates are not just flat plates, they have bulging "roots" which anchor them in place.

To make matters even worse, at the present time the continents are not moving as expected. In some places, they are moving as the theory predicts, but in some places they are going in the opposite direction. Perhaps major movement has stopped. Are these just leftover movements? Did it happen in the past? How can you move a continent?

It seems what is needed is a major event, operating at energy levels far greater than those seen today. It would also have to be global in nature.

Could the flood of Noah's day have been the event which separated the continents? Could they have separated in the past with rates much greater than present rates and now they pretty much have come to a halt?

How can we explain the huge zones of metamorphic rock frequently underlying the blanket of sedimentary rock on the surface? We know that rock adjacent to a fault can be metamorphosed by the heat and pressure generated there. The minerals present in the original rock can be recrystallized into new mineral combinations. But how can such conditions apply over incredibly large zones, thousands of feet deep and hundreds of miles wide?

VIII. METAMORPHISM OF ROCKS

Does it Take a Long Time?

The huge deposits of metamorphic rock are so unlike rock which forms today that it is nearly impossible to imagine how it could be accomplished.

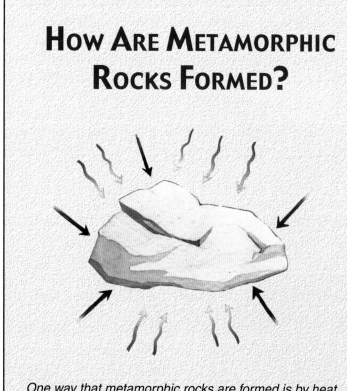

HOW ARE METAMORPHIC ROCKS FORMED?

One way that metamorphic rocks are formed is by heat and pressure recrystallizing the minerals in rock into new mineral combinations.

Those who claim the earth has been here for millions or billions of years usually claim that deep burial of sedimentary rock is accompanied by sustained high pressures and temperatures, causing various atoms to be replaced or recombined into different mineral and crystal forms.

Usually they refer to a series of minerals, (containing atoms of iron, magnesium, potassium, aluminum, silicon, and oxygen) noting variations in the composition of these minerals and attributing these differences to greater or lesser intense conditions. If you start with solid rock, with mineral grains already well formed, it seemingly would take a long time to change them.

Let's Look Again

Other researchers have noted some problems with this story about the unobserved past. They note that in the laboratory each of these minerals can be made to form or recrystallize in just a few days, even with more normal temperatures and pressures. By starting with a watery mineral gel, the reaction of transformation and grain growth is even more rapid.

When metamorphic rocks are studied under a microscope, minerals of supposedly different metamorphic origins are sometimes found right next to one another. How could regional conditions be responsible? Obviously the standard view of high pressure and high temperature

There are problems with the theory of heat and pressure over long periods of time when explaining large areas of metamorphic rock. Variations in minerals, the need for heat, and other problems can be explained by a catastrophic event, such as a worldwide flood.

LONG TIME   **VERSUS**   **CATASTROPHE**

conditions applied regionally over a long period of time can't be right.

To explain what is seen, some have proposed that variations in the original sediments would lead to different minerals. Finer grain size would also speed up the metamorphic reaction, as would the presence of hot water permeating the sediments. Perhaps if the sediments had not yet hardened into

rock the reaction could take place quickly, at more normal conditions.

This subject still needs a lot of research, but the requirements fit the idea of rapid sedimentation, deep burial, and major tectonic forces acting during a brief time. The long time idea doesn't seem to work as well.

IX. RADIOISOTOPE DECAY

Atoms make up everything in creation, whether solid, liquid, or gas. Each atom has different properties. Some are heavier than others and some, especially the heavier ones, are unstable, decaying into smaller more stable ones. We call these unstable atoms radioactive.

Uranium Decay

The most well-known radioactive atom is uranium, which occurs in several different forms or isotopes. One of those isotopes, uranium 238, decays into thorium 234, which itself is unstable and decays into a smaller atom which is unstable, too. This process continues until finally the atom

changes into lead 206, which decays no more. In this case, the uranium would be called the parent atom, and the lead called the daughter atom.

These heavy radioactive atoms are concentrated in the earth's crust, with much fewer of them being found in the mantle and none in the core. As each one decays, it gives off heat. While the heat derived from one atom's decay is not much, the atoms occur in clusters of billions and billions and the total amount of heat given off actually contributes to the earth's underground heat.

Nuclear power plants use a radioactive source which is highly concentrated, so that the heat becomes intense. They capture this heat and use it to generate electricity.

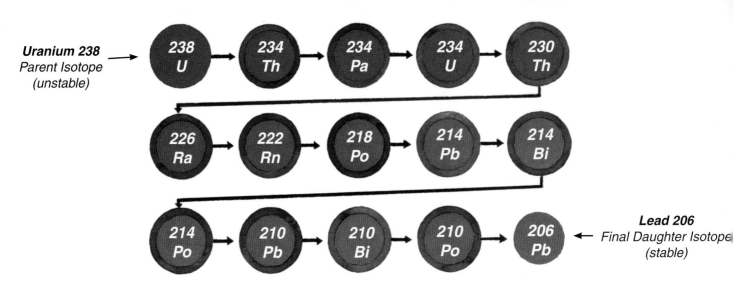

| 238 U | → | 234 Th | → | 234 Pa | → | 234 U | → | 230 Th |

Uranium 238
Parent Isotope (unstable)

| 226 Ra | → | 222 Rn | → | 218 Po | → | 214 Pb | → | 214 Bi |

| 214 Po | → | 210 Pb | → | 210 Bi | → | 210 Po | → | 206 Pb |

Lead 206
Final Daughter Isotope (stable)

Radioisotope Dating

Sometimes this process of atomic decay is used in an attempt to determine how old an object is. It involves very precise measurements and very complicated mathematics, but it's not very hard to understand.

Isotopes are slightly different atoms of an element. If we know how fast a particular isotope of one element (the parent) changes into an isotope of another element (the daughter), and can measure how much of each is present in an object, we can calculate how long it would take for that amount of parent isotope to change into that amount of daughter isotope. (At least that's what the theory says.)

Because uranium 238 is unstable, the isotope will keep changing into unstable isotopes of other elements until it finally turns into lead which is stable (above). Radioisotope dating works by measuring the amount of uranium 238 and its daughter isotopes that are present in a rock. Since we know how fast the isotopes decay, then an approximate age should be able to be found.

Carbon Dating

The carbon-dating technique cannot be used to date rocks or most fossils, but it can be used to date things that were once living — things that contain carbon. Here's how it works. Sometimes nitrogen 14 changes into carbon 14 high in the atmosphere. Over time, however, the carbon 14 decays back into nitrogen 14. Since plants "breathe" carbon dioxide, their leaves, stems, and seeds contain some carbon 14 in their structures along with the more common isotope,

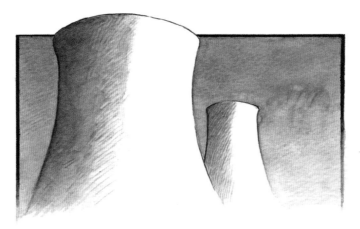

Nuclear power plants use the unstable qualities of uranium to produce large amounts of heat to generate electricity.

carbon 12. Once they stop living, they stop taking in new carbon 14 and the unstable carbon 14 already there begins to decay back into nitrogen 14, while the stable carbon 12 remains. By measuring the amount of carbon 14 left sometime after the plant dies, you can calculate (in theory) how long ago the plant died. Since animals eat plants, their deaths can be dated in the same way.

From measurements, we know this rate of decay. It decays fast enough that all of it would be gone in 50,000 years or so. But, in reality, because carbon 14 decays so rapidly, it is not very useful for dating things more than a few thousand years old. Beyond that, no one trusts it because such tiny amounts are left, and accuracy problems are so numerous. Even for dates within the last 3,000 years, archaeologists like to have some known historical date to check it with. For things older than that, they seldom trust it at all.

The Dating of Rocks

Over the years, several of these decaying isotopes of radioactive atoms have been used in an attempt to date rocks. It's important to know that they are only useful for dating igneous rocks, rocks that used to be in a hot liquid condition. They cannot be used to date fossil-bearing

Have Decay Rates Changed?

What if the rate of decay of parent into daughter changes? What if it was different in the past? Just because it doesn't change today, are we correct in assuming that it did not change in the past?

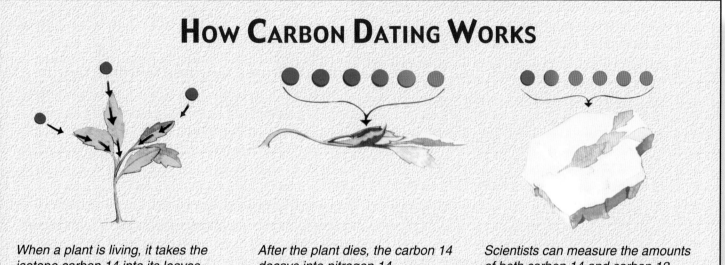

HOW CARBON DATING WORKS

When a plant is living, it takes the isotope carbon 14 into its leaves, stems, and seeds.

After the plant dies, the carbon 14 decays into nitrogen 14.

Scientists can measure the amounts of both carbon 14 and carbon 12. Since they know the time it takes the isotope to decay, they can calculate when the plant died.

sedimentary rock because sedimentary rocks are made up of pieces of previous rocks that have been eroded, transported, and redeposited. By dating the minerals of the sedimentary rock, you would really be dating the minerals of a previous rock. Since the material would be all mixed up and strewn around, no useful date would be obtained.

The most often used radioisotope dating techniques are uranium 238 to lead 206, potassium 40 into argon 40, and rubidium 87 into strontium 87.

Obviously, the dating of rocks would only be accurate if certain conditions are met.

For dating samples, scientists use precise instruments to measure the amount of elements.

For some of the radioactive isotopes, the decay rate does change. But for those that have been used for dating methods, the rate is pretty constant. Scientists have tried for many years, in many ways, to make the decay rates change, but under normal circumstances they seem to be pretty uniform.

And now they are finding some ways to change them, and there are some strong hints that the rates may have changed in the past. It looks like things may have been different for short periods in the past. More research will tell us a lot.

What If the Amounts Have Changed?

What if over the entire history of the rock, something has happened that would add some of the parent or maybe take away some of the parent. Perhaps some of the daughter has been added or taken away. Unless we knew how much they changed, the calculated age would be misleading.

There are many ways in which either parent or daughter atoms can be added to or taken away from a rock. The most important is the presence of water. Water can dissolve either uranium or lead, and transport them elsewhere, and if it has done so, the calculated date would be in error.

It is extremely unlikely that a rock would remain totally isolated for long periods of time, especially if major flooding took place. What rock could possibly be isolated from the waters of a flood or even from the water percolating through the ground?

What If Some Daughter Was Present at the Start?

Radioisotope dating theory claims to calculate how long ago a hot liquid lava cooled into a solid rock. Obviously, the liquid material existed before and would contain both parent and daughter, such as potassium 40 and argon 40. The thinking is, however, that when in liquid form, the gas argon can bubble out and everything that is left is thoroughly mixed. Once the rock solidifies, then the gas can no longer bubble out and the amount of argon begins to build up as potassium decays. In this way, those studying the rock can determine how much argon was there at the start and how much got there through decay, or at least they claim they can.

In reality, it is not so easy. The rock which formed at the eruption of Mount St. Helens in 1980 contained much argon, even though it should have contained none. In fact, one of its minerals "dated" at 2.8 million years, when it was only 15 years old. Volcanic rock formed in the recent eruptions of Hawaiian volcanoes dates at 30 million years old. Many other faulty dating attempts could be cited. Obviously, original argon is frequently contained in rocks, and researchers cannot tell original from daughter, leading to false "ages."

A Further Problem

When the same rock is dated by more than one method, it will often yield different "ages." And when the rock is dated more than one time by the same method, it will often give different results.

Rocks that were created during and since the 1980 eruption of Mount St. Helens (below) "dated" up to 2.8 million years old.

THREE POSSIBLE PROBLEMS OF DATING

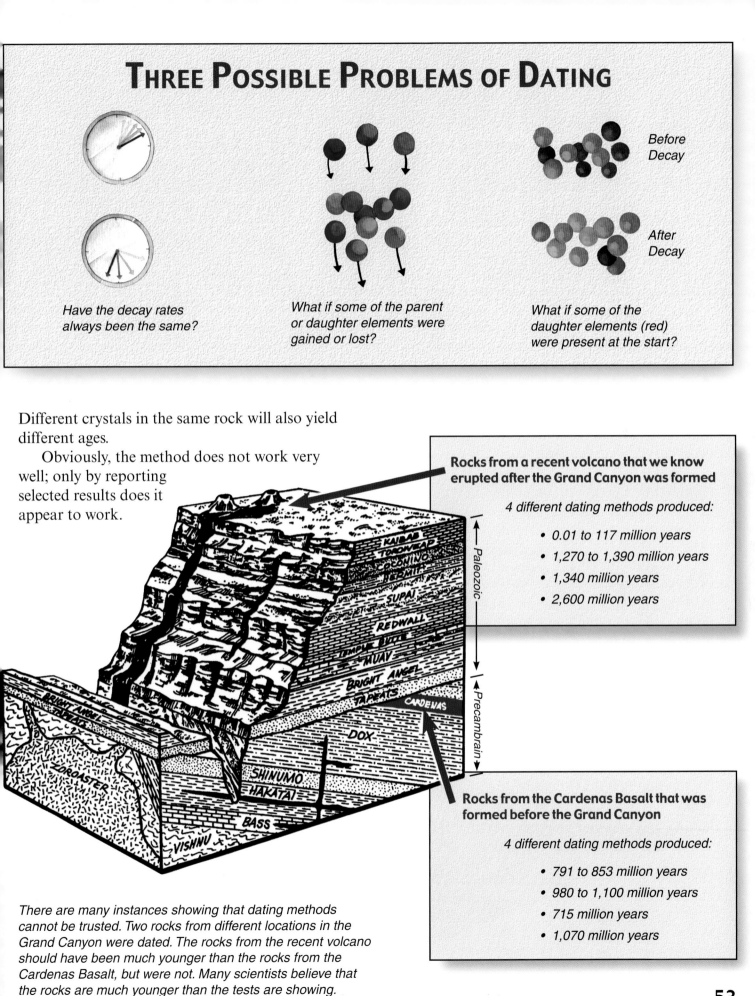

Have the decay rates always been the same?

What if some of the parent or daughter elements were gained or lost?

Before Decay

After Decay

What if some of the daughter elements (red) were present at the start?

Different crystals in the same rock will also yield different ages.

Obviously, the method does not work very well; only by reporting selected results does it appear to work.

Rocks from a recent volcano that we know erupted after the Grand Canyon was formed

4 different dating methods produced:

- 0.01 to 117 million years
- 1,270 to 1,390 million years
- 1,340 million years
- 2,600 million years

Rocks from the Cardenas Basalt that was formed before the Grand Canyon

4 different dating methods produced:

- 791 to 853 million years
- 980 to 1,100 million years
- 715 million years
- 1,070 million years

There are many instances showing that dating methods cannot be trusted. Two rocks from different locations in the Grand Canyon were dated. The rocks from the recent volcano should have been much younger than the rocks from the Cardenas Basalt, but were not. Many scientists believe that the rocks are much younger than the tests are showing.

Chapter 5

WAYS TO DATE THE ENTIRE EARTH

S ince dating rocks is full of possible errors, due to the fact that material existed before the rock and that the rock's makeup can be changed even after it is formed, can we devise a better way to date the earth?

Is There a Way to Date the Entire Earth?

This would solve many problems because, obviously, you can hardly change the makeup of

By summing up all the ways that salt enters and leaves the ocean, and measuring the amount of salt in the ocean now, scientists can approximate the maximum age of the ocean, and thus the earth.

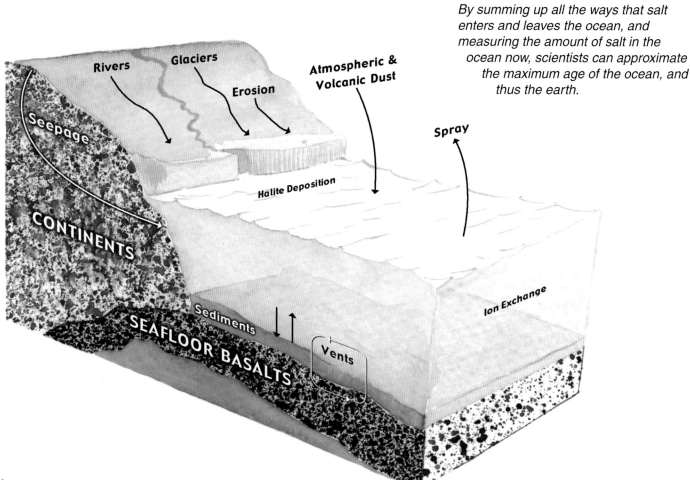

Scientists can date the earth by measuring the total volume of the continents and how fast the sediments eroding from the continents enter the ocean.

the entire earth. As it turns out, there are many ways to date the earth, its oceans, or its atmosphere, and these appear to be more accurate than dating an individual rock.

Chemicals in the Ocean

The ocean contains many chemicals dissolved in the seawater. Rivers bring even more of the chemicals into the ocean on a daily basis. We can measure how fast the chemicals are added and we know how much of the chemicals are in the ocean. Therefore, we can calculate how long it would take for that much chemical to build up at the current rate of addition. This would yield an age for the ocean.

For instance, we know that the ocean contains a great deal of salt. By summing up all the possible ways in which salt can be added to the ocean, and all the possible ways that salt can be removed from the ocean, and knowing how much salt is in the ocean, we can discern its apparent age. When we do, we see that the ocean could not possibly be any older than 62 million years. This is not to say that the ocean is 62 million years old, but that it could not be any older than that. Theories of evolution, however, assume that the oceans have been salty for at least 3 billion years. But if they were that old, and had been receiving salt all that time, they

would be so full of salt that life in them would be impossible. Therefore, they just could not be very old. Obviously, dating the world's oceans is a more reliable technique than dating an individual rock which can be changed by more recent processes. And here is another thought — if the oceans were to have had some salt at the start or if some major flooding event added much more salt to it at one time in the past, the maximum "age" would be even less.

Calculations based on dozens of other chemicals being added to the ocean yield similar dates.

Erosion of the Continents

Likewise, we can measure the total volume of the continents and we can measure how fast sediments eroding from the continents enter the ocean.

At the present rate of erosion, the continents will all be gone in 15 million years. This includes any possible addition to the continents by uplift and addition of new materials by volcanic eruptions.

Again, this is not to say that the continents are 15 million years old, but that they cannot be any older than this. However, evolution theory assumes that the continents are much, much older. Obviously, such assumptions cannot be right.

By measuring the amount of sediments on the ocean floor, it can be determined how long it would take the rivers of the world to deposit them.

Once again, however, we must consider the possibility of processes operating at different rates in the past. Perhaps the continents rose rapidly in the more recent past. If so, the approximate age would need drastic revision downwards.

Sediments in the Ocean

A similar calculation concludes that the sediments which are presently found on the ocean floor would have been deposited by our present-day rivers in 14 million years. This calculation includes every possible way that the sediment can be removed from the ocean by other means. Thus, the oceans could not possibly be any older than 14 million years.

Again, if major flooding occurred and added sediment to the ocean at rates greater than at present, then the maximum age would be much younger.

Dating the Atmosphere

Helium, a lightweight gas, exists in our atmosphere. We can measure how much is there. We can also measure how much helium enters the atmosphere from the crust of the earth. We also know how much helium is leaving the atmosphere by drifting into space.

As it turns out, all of the helium that is now in the atmosphere would have gotten there at present rates of addition in less than 2 million years. Again, what if an event like a major flood happened which released more of the helium from the crust? The maximum age would be reduced even further.

Dating the Magnetic Field

The earth's magnetic field is due to currents of electricity in the metallic outer core of the earth. The magnetic field protects the earth from harmful cosmic rays, in addition to causing our compass needles to point north.

The strength of the earth's magnetic field has been accurately measured for over 160 years and it is seen to be declining. At the present rate of decline, it will rather soon be too weak to provide any beneficial protection for living things. On the other hand, if it has always been declining at this rate, just 10,000 years ago it would have been too strong for life to exist. There is some evidence that the magnetic field has reversed in the past, with compass needles pointing south. Scientists do not have a good theory as to how this might have happened, but the most likely theory is that rapid movement of the metallic minerals in the outer core has caused rapid flip-flops in the magnetic field. A similar flip-flop happens today in an electromagnet such as in your car's alternator. The flip-flopping would occur even though the total magnetic field continued to decay. In fact, it would cause the magnetic field to decay even more rapidly. Now movements in the core have slowed down and practically halted, allowing the magnetic field to return to its normal condition in which it is merely deteriorating.

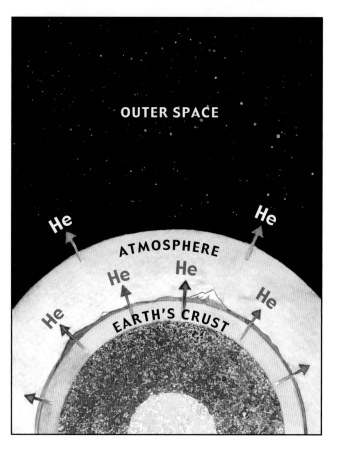

Scientists can measure the amount of helium in the atmosphere. Since they know the rate at which helium is being released from the crust and how much is being lost into space, a maximum age for the earth's atmosphere can be found.

Conclusion

Dating individual rocks can sometimes lead to faulty conclusions. The better dating techniques, however, involve dating the entire earth's systems and are based on a long period of measurement. The best geologic evidence and even evidence from other areas of science seem to indicate that the earth is not nearly as old as many people believe.

Dating the Magnetic Field

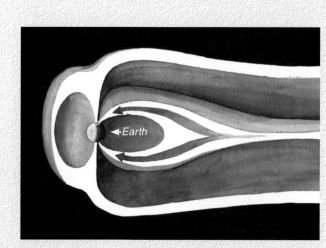

Accurate measurements taken for over 160 years have shown the strength of earth's magnetic field to be declining. At the current rate of decline, the magnetic field would have been too strong for life to exist on earth as little as 10,000 years ago.

Year	Field Strength	Year	Field Strength
1835	8.558 *	1945	8.090
1845	8.488	1955	8.035
1880	8.363	1955	8.067
1880	8.336	1958	8.038
1885	8.347	1959	8.086
1885	8.375	1960	8.053
1905	8.291	1960	8.037
1915	8.225	1960	8.025
1922	8.165	1965	8.013
1925	8.149	1965	8.017
1935	8.088		
1942	8.009	* measured in amp-meter^2 X 10^{22}	
1945	8.065		
1945	8.010		
1945	8.066		

Chapter 6

GREAT GEOLOGIC EVENTS OF THE PAST

Geologic events today are rather ordinary and predictable, in accordance with the scientific laws which we observe. What if there were events in the past which were so different that they involved processes at rates, scales, and intensities far beyond what we observe today? Furthermore, what if there were some events which involved entirely different scientific principles than are in operation today?

The Bible actually mentions three such events, each one of which would have accomplished great geologic work. If, when trying to understand the earth's past, we ignore them in our thinking, we will probably come to faulty conclusions.

I. CREATION

The Bible tells us that "In the beginning God created the heaven and the earth" (Gen. 1:1).

God created a perfect world in only six days (left).

In God's wisdom, He did not give us all of the details as to the nature of "the earth" when it was first created, but it does give a few clues.

DAY 1

Creation of light on newly created earth (right)

The Processes of Creation

Today, an important scientific law has been discovered. In fact, it is perhaps the most important and best-proven scientific law. It is often called the first law of science.

This basic law says that in the present world nothing is being created out of nothing. It also says that nothing that exists can be uncreated — that is, go out of existence. Thus, creation from nothing is scientifically impossible. But yet, creation is here.

From this we can conclude that when God did create, He was using processes which we do not observe. The Bible also tells us that at the end of the sixth day of creation, God "rested" from all the work, which He had created (Gen. 2:2). With the exception of the supernatural biblical miracles performed by Jesus Christ and others, even God is no longer creating. It appears that God passed that first law of science at the end of creation week. Now all of His creation obeys that first law. The process of creation is over.

DAY 2 — Separation Of Waters

What Was the World Like in the Beginning?

The second verse of Genesis 1 tells us that the earth was in a watery state. Perhaps this was just the ocean covering the entire crust, with the earliest rocks of each continent fully covered. Perhaps there was no solid material at all.

At least we know that on day three of creation week God called the ocean waters together into one place and the dry land appeared (Gen. 1:9). At this point the continents took shape in a form that we would recognize.

DAY 3 — Dry Land and Plants

No doubt rocks were present. Certainly the cores of the continents were present, probably largely made up of granite.

A process is also hinted at in the formation of the continents. The Bible does not say that God just spoke and the continents sprang into existence, but implies that the continents were uplifted and the waters drained off into the newly formed ocean basins.

Keep in mind that present-day laws may not have been in operation, but certainly gravity in some form was operating. If so, there would be sediments eroded and redeposited in low places as the waters drained off. But these sediments would have no trace of life, because life was not created until after the continents were in place.

Today, life exists everywhere on planet Earth, in the oceans, on the land, in the air. No sediments are deposited today which have no traces of life. Yet we see much sedimentary rock which is completely void of fossils. Could these fossil-free layers of rock be the result of events early on day three of creation week? These would be a wonderful provision to the earth once it was completed, providing aquifers for springs and underground water, as well as nutrient-rich soils in which plants could grow.

DAY 4 —
Sun and
Moon

Days Four, Five, and Six

On day four, God created the sun, which would bathe the earth in its solar energy, and the moon, with a gravitational force providing the ocean tides, continually cleansing and renewing the earth's oceans (Gen. 1:14-19).

On days five and six, He created animal life and man, placed them all in His beautiful garden, and pronounced the result to be "very good," exactly as He wanted. Both the action of burrowing animals and the roots of plants would accomplish geologic work (Gen. 1:11-12, 20-25).

The Water Cycle

The Bible also tells us that in the original earth the weather and river systems which we have today were not in operation. Rivers were fed by huge underground sources of water (Gen. 2:10). It may not have rained then as it does now, but a heavy dew watered the plants (Gen. 2:5-6).

Natural Resources

The Bible describes the newly created land as quite beautiful with abundant gold and precious stones (Gen. 2:11-12). These must have been created by God to meet the needs of mankind in His "very good" earth (Gen. 1:31).

DAYS 5, 6 —
Animal Life

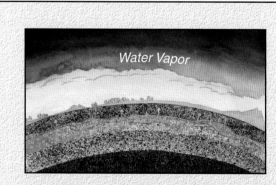

THE WATER CYCLE

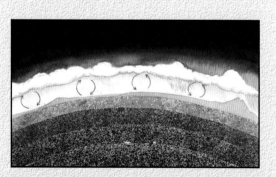

Before the flood, it is believed that there was a dense cloud of water vapor that surrounded the earth and also a great deal of water underground. The dew watered the plants, and underground springs fed rivers and streams.

After the flood, water evaporates from the oceans and rivers and then returns to the earth as rain. The rain waters the plants and the runoff feeds most rivers and streams.

Even though the earth was created "very good" and God's intention was that it would last forever, things did not last. Adam and Eve disobeyed God's authority. Disobedience is sin, and "the wages of sin is death" (Rom. 6:23).

In Genesis 3 we see that the entire creation came

After man's sin of disobedience, the whole world was cursed and Adam and Eve were cast from the garden. The world experienced death and decay for the first time.

under the curse of sin, because of Adam and Eve's rebellion. Plants were cursed (verse 18); the animals were cursed (verse 14); mankind was cursed (verse 15–17, 19). Even the entire earth was cursed (verse 17). The apostle Paul said that the "whole creation groaneth and travaileth in pain together until now" (Rom. 8:22). Because of the presence of sin and its penalty, death, everything decays and dies. Not only do all life forms die, but the sun is burning out, the moon's orbit is

decaying, and even atoms are unstable. Everywhere we look, we see the horrible penalty of sin.

The marvelous balance of nature maintains the earth's systems to a wonderful degree, but still everything is in the process of wearing down.

The Second Law of Science

Scientists have observed that in every process or reaction in the universe the components deteriorate. Every experiment has verified the truthfulness of this statement. Through much study and observation, scientists were able to state this decay tendency in a scientific law now recognized as the second most important law in science.

Everywhere We Look

Where could we look on the planet Earth and see things not affected by the curse of death on all creation, as described in this law of science? We certainly see it in living creatures where every animal and person grows old and eventually dies. We see it every time mutations alter the genetic code causing a loss of genetic information (never the production of new and better information as evolution requires).

In the non-living world, we see energy losses due to friction in every moving part. This is why no perpetual motion machine is possible. We never see a perfect crystal, nor do we ever see a uranium atom form by itself, we only see them deteriorate.

DAY 6 — *Man*

Adam and Eve lived in a perfect world in the Garden of Eden.

Science and the Bible

Thus, we see that the two great laws of science exactly represent the two great events of early history. The first law of science, which states that nothing is now being created nor destroyed, exactly represents the Genesis doctrine of the finished creation, which God maintains. The second law of science says that this once "very good" creation now suffers under the penalty of sin and death. Every object on earth that we study and every reaction that we observe abides by these two laws. Our observations agree with what we read in the Bible.

III. The Flood

Even though ruined by sin's principle of death and decay, the beautiful world created by God still continued in a wonderful state of equilibrium until Noah's day. But God's very nature demands that sin be punished, and the flood was His method of punishment on the rebellious civilization in the days of Noah.

The flood totally destroyed that beautiful pre-flood world. We are told that after Noah's family and all the animals were on board the ark, in "the same day were all the fountains of the great deep broken up and the windows of heaven were opened and the rain was upon the earth forty days and forty nights" (Gen. 7:11–12).

These conditions prevailed for another hundred and fifty days (verse 24) until "the fountains also of the deep and the windows of heaven were stopped and the rain from heaven was restrained" (Gen. 8:2)

While the earth was undergoing a major catastrophe that would reshape the world, God kept His people safe in the ark.

From these bare facts we can discern the basic nature of the flood, but still the total effects are beyond our understanding.

The First 40 Days

On day two of creation week, God had placed a great deal of water above the atmosphere (Gen. 1:7). During the flood the windows of heaven were opened and a special rain, worldwide in scope, poured down on the earth for 40 days and 40 nights. Can you imagine the erosion that would result from this torrential worldwide rainfall? Think of the extensive deposition of eroded sediments. While we understand the processes of erosion and deposition today, during the flood these intense processes were operating on a scale far beyond what we experience now. The layer of atmospheric water, probably in the form of invisible gaseous water vapor, condensed into liquid and fell as rain. No doubt this water contributed to the waters of the flood, but it is unlikely that this alone would provide enough to cover the mountains.

The "fountains of the great deep" might be best understood as great volcanoes and springs on the ocean floor. These would have erupted great volumes of lava and water into the ocean and steam into the atmosphere above. The heat and dust particles would have caused the atmospheric water to condense and begin to fall. The steam rising into the atmosphere would have allowed the rain to pour down in this intense fashion for 40 days and 40 nights, and then continue for the next 110 days.

Tsunamis (or tidal waves) resulting from these dynamic underwater events would have caused great walls of water to race from the ocean to the continents. The energy of these waves would first

SOURCES OF FLOOD WATER

"The windows of heaven," were probably a result of a layer of water vapor that surrounded the earth condensing and falling as a worldwide rain.

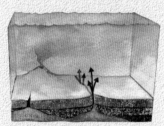

"The fountains of the great deep" were evidently great volcanoes and springs on the ocean floor.

The convulsions of the earth would probably have resulted in the **rising of the ocean basins** forcing the water onto the continents.

erode the land to a flat surface and then deposit sediments on top. It would push the ocean waters farther and farther onto the continents, mixing with the runoff of the intense rainfall. Nothing could withstand the force of these waters.

HOW THE FLOOD MIGHT HAVE SHAPED THE LAND

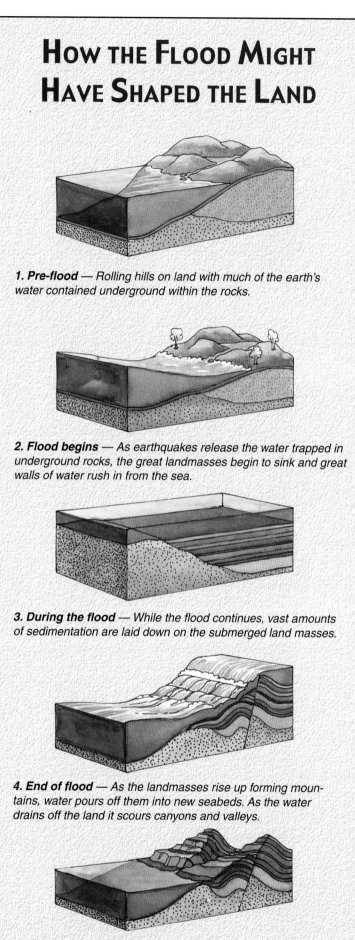

1. Pre-flood — *Rolling hills on land with much of the earth's water contained underground within the rocks.*

2. Flood begins — *As earthquakes release the water trapped in underground rocks, the great landmasses begin to sink and great walls of water rush in from the sea.*

3. During the flood — *While the flood continues, vast amounts of sedimentation are laid down on the submerged land masses.*

4. End of flood — *As the landmasses rise up forming mountains, water pours off them into new seabeds. As the water drains off the land it scours canyons and valleys.*

5. The earth today — *As erosion continues we see more and more evidence of a great flood.*

We may see some faint reminders of these fountains of the great deep in modern-day springs in the ocean bottom. These bring up super-heated waters laden with a variety of chemicals, which are deposited on the sea floor as the hot waters encounter the cold ocean waters.

The convulsions of the earth during the flood would probably have caused the ocean basins themselves to rise, providing still more water which inundated the land. By the end of the first 40 days, probably the entire world had been covered by water.

The Waters "Prevailed"

"And the waters prevailed and were increased greatly upon the earth: and the ark went upon the face of the waters and the waters prevailed

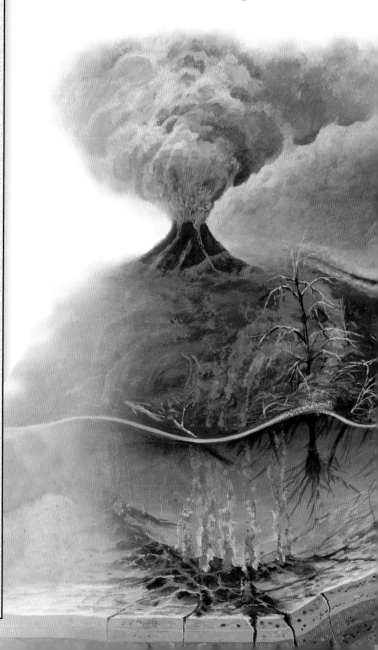

exceedingly upon the earth: and all the high hills, that were under the whole heaven, were covered. Fifteen cubits upward did the waters prevail; and the mountains were covered and all flesh died that moved upon the earth, both fowl, and of cattle, and of beast, and of every creeping thing that creepeth upon the earth, and every man: all in whose nostrils was the breath of life, of all that was in the dry land, died" (Gen. 7:18–22).

For 150 days the waters prevailed upon the earth. With waters going back and forth eroding and redepositing, the sediments would be interbedded with volcanic sediments as well as minerals and metals and salts brought up by the fountains of the great deep.

The plants and animals that died in this flood either floated to the surface, or were trapped in the sediments and buried. These were fossilized as the sediments hardened into sedimentary rock.

The ark came to rest on the mountains of Ararat after 150 days.

The Draining of the Waters

"And God made a wind to pass over the earth, and the waters assuaged; the fountains also of the deep and the windows of heaven were stopped, and the rain from heaven was restrained; and the waters returned from off the earth continually" (Gen. 8:1–3). At the end of the 150 days, the waters began to run off the continents back into the ocean and the ark came to rest on the mountains of Ararat. For the next several months the survivors stayed on the ark as Noah sent out the raven and the dove to test the water level. Finally, the ground at the base of the mountain was dry enough, so they left the ark to begin their new life.

There is certainly enough water on planet Earth to cover the entire globe. If the earth were a completely smooth sphere with no oceans and no mountains, the water would stand at a depth of about 8,500 feet (2,591 m). Today most of the water is in the oceans which still cover over two-thirds of the globe.

In order to drain the flood waters, several things must have happened, the most important being the deepening and widening of the ocean basins into which the waters could flow. If the continents were once connected, this must have been the time when they separated. The sediments on the continents would have been deposited during the first six months, and now they separated

The earth suffered violent volcanic convulsions and rock movements so that major reforming of the continents took place during the flood.

Some scientists believe that it might have been a meteorite shower that triggered the flood.

with parts of the sedimentary layers on either side of the enlarging ocean.

The continental separation would have been accompanied by ocean basin sinking as well as spreading.

Into these deep and wide ocean basins the water began to drain, leaving the continents high and dry. It would have taken several months for the waters to drain off as is recorded in Genesis 8.

Meanwhile, the continents themselves were uplifting. The sedimentary and granitic rocks beneath would be less dense than the surrounding basaltic rock, and the continents would tend to bulge up several thousand feet. As the continents uplifted and shifted, many mountain chains would buckle up. These mountains would not have existed before the flood. They are made of once-flat-lying sediments deposited at the bottom of the flood ocean, but now wrinkled up to form mountains. This is why we find ocean fossils near the top of Mount Everest, 29,000 feet (8,839 m) in elevation, the highest point on earth.

As the continents rose, much of the flood waters would have been trapped in interior lakes. We know that Great Salt Lake in Utah is a small

remnant of Lake Bonneville, a much bigger lake, which was left over from the flood. There is evidence of quite a number of other inland lakes in the western United States, including Lake Manly of modern-day Death Valley, and Canyonlands Lake and Hopi Lake upriver from what is now the Grand Canyon.

Geologists have found evidence that great meteorites or comets were blasting into the earth at about this time. It makes sense that earth was bombarded by meteorites since the moon contains evidence of many meteorite impacts as do the earth's neighbors, Mars and Venus. Perhaps the entire inner solar system was passing through an asteroid belt prepared by God to contribute to the destruction of the earth. Since most of these meteorites which fell on earth would have fallen in the water, they would leave no trace, but quite a few traces have been seen on or near the present-day land surface.

Once the year of the flood was over and Noah's family and the animals started their new life, the earth was very different. Plants would have begun to sprout worldwide and animals would have migrated to their new homes over the next centuries, but it probably took several hundred years for the earth to settle back down into the equilibrium we enjoy now. The centuries to follow would be marked by intense storms, continual earthquakes and volcanoes, perhaps meteorite impacts, etc. We can be quite thankful that the earth has calmed down to be our present wonderful home.

After the land had dried enough to support Noah's family and the animals, they left the ark and made an altar unto the Lord.

IV. The Ice Age

Consider the state of the world immediately after the flood. The waters of the ocean would be quite warm, having been heated by the hot sub-surface liquids brought up by the great "fountains of the deep." Volcanoes would add still more heat, as would the friction of moving continents. Estimates

During the Ice Age, a glacier extended down into the present day United States (above). Conditions were so harsh in parts of the world that even the woolly mammoth could not survive (right).

are that the world's oceans were quite a bit warmer than our present-day oceans. As is the case today, the warmer the water, the more the evaporation. Thus, these warm oceans would have resulted in a great deal of water evaporated into the atmosphere.

Meantime, the continents would be rather cold with essentially nothing growing there. Certainly small plants would begin to grow as soon as they could, but there were no forests. The ground surface in many places was little more than saturated mud.

The atmosphere also was quite different. The continental uplifts and volcanoes would have placed a great deal of volcanic dust in the atmosphere which would affect the world's weather. While this cloud of dust would not make the world completely dark, it would tend to reflect much of the sun's warming sunlight back into space. The saturated ground surface would do likewise.

A Build-up of Ice on the Continents

The effect of all these factors would have been dramatic. The difference in temperature between the warm oceans and the cold continents would have caused great air movements from the oceans to the continents. The excessive moisture contained in the warm air would have condensed and fallen as snow on the cold continents, particularly towards the polar regions. Studies have shown there would be almost a continual snowfall for centuries following the flood. During the summer the snow would tend not to melt because of less solar heating. The snow would pack down into ice and begin to spread out as a large continental glacier. This condition would continue until the oceans gave up their excess heat and the atmosphere was cleansed of its volcanic debris.

A Large Polar Ice Cap

The Ice Age was not a time when the entire globe was covered with ice. However, the polar ice caps were much larger with the glaciers extending down into the United States and Europe. In regions farther south like Mexico and Egypt the conditions were quite lovely,

As a glacier moves across the land, rock debris in the bottom of it scratches the bedrock below leaving streaks called striations (above). A valley glacier in Antarctica can be seen moving down the center of the photo (below).

with cooler temperatures than at present and abundant rainfall. This "Ice Age" probably lasted 600 to 1,000 years — approximately between the time of Noah and Abraham.

Glacial Erosion and Deposition

As the continental glacier spread over Canada and into the United States, it would have easily eroded the soft sediments recently deposited by the flood. In places, it may have even scoured these off down to bedrock. Today much of Canada's surface is made up of granitic rocks covered by a thin layer of glacial soil. Often the rocks which are exposed have streaks in them called striations. These were formed as the glacier and the rocks it carried scraped the rocks over which they flowed.

The glaciers would trap much of this eroded material in the ice. As the ice melted, it would leave behind huge quantities of chipped-off rock and soil. Today this soil forms great fertile valleys and the rocks are stacked in boulder fields called moraines.

Fossilization of Land Animals

Most fossils are of sea creatures. They were mostly deposited by the flood of Noah's day. In northern latitudes many of these fossil deposits are covered by a thin layer of soil and frozen tundra in which are buried many land animals, like mammoths and mastodons. These were animals which descended from those on board Noah's ark and migrated into northern regions. They lived in great herds and died in large numbers in local storms and devastating events during the Ice Age.

On occasion some of these mammoths are found partially frozen. While there are large numbers of mammoth bones, only a few dozen mammoths have been found frozen either partially or completely. These extremely rare events would take rare circumstances, happening on occasion during this terrible Ice Age.

Glaciers Today

The polar ice caps today are much smaller than they were during the Ice Age. Even in tall mountains we see evidence that greater glaciers were there in the past. Glaciers typically erode a U-shaped valley quite different from the V-shaped valleys eroded by rivers. From these clues we can put together an idea of what the Ice Age was like.

Chapter 7

QUESTIONS PEOPLE ASK

How Was the Grand Canyon Formed?

Many geologists now recognize that the Colorado River could never have carved the 18-mile-wide Grand Canyon. That kind of canyon requires a great deal of rapidly flowing water able to continually remove the eroded materials taking them far downstream, allowing the water to erode even more deeply. Slow erosion will not do the job.

Today, the Colorado River flows southerly along the uplifted Kaibab Upwarp and suddenly takes a right-hand turn through the mountain, forming the canyon. What would cause a river to flow directly through a mountain? Rivers usually go around mountains.

At the end of Noah's flood it appears that a great volume of water was trapped, held in place by the Kaibab Upwarp. Ice Age rains filled the lake to overflowing and as it burst through its mountain "dam," the huge volume of lake waters carved the canyon.

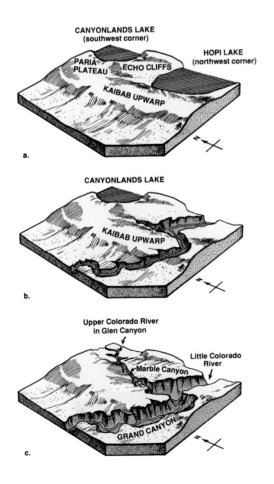

Marble Canyon (above) and the Grand Canyon were most likely formed by a build up of flood water in huge lakes (a) that burst through the plateau, carving out the canyons (b and c).

What Causes the Geysers in Yellowstone Park?

Volcanism continued at an intense rate for several centuries following Noah's flood. The series of volcanic eruptions at Yellowstone was perhaps one of the very greatest.

At Yellowstone Park, the soil and rock is thin, allowing very hot material to be near the surface. As rain and run-off water trickle down into the earth they get heated, bubbling up in places as hot springs. In some places the underground water is trapped and when heated to an excessive degree, it bursts out in a geyser. The geyser stops once the pressure is relieved, but will erupt again as building pressures exceed the maximum.

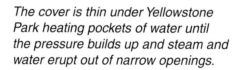

The cover is thin under Yellowstone Park heating pockets of water until the pressure builds up and steam and water erupt out of narrow openings.

How Did Niagara Falls Form?

The level of water in Lake Erie is somewhat higher than the elevation of nearby Lake Ontario. A river draining the waters of Lake Erie into Lake Ontario runs over the Niagara escarpment, resulting in a spectacular set of falls. Erosion takes place as the water roars over the falls, and the escarpment naturally recedes toward Lake Erie at the rate of four to five feet (1.2 to 1.5 m) per year. Over the years, it has formed a seven-mile-long (3.7 km) gorge between the falls and Lake Ontario. Simple division indicates that the fall and gorge system is only a few thousand years old. Thankfully, engineers have been able to control the erosion, and the falls are stable today.

Why Are the Appalachian and Rocky Mountains So Different?

Both mountain chains are the result of layers of sediments deposited by Noah's flood. The Appalachians buckled up in the early stages of the flood and were subjected to massive erosion by the continuing flood waters. The Rocky Mountains buckled up late in the flood, extending up above the flood waters as the waters drained off. Thus, the erosion to which they were subjected was much less intense.

Niagara Falls is a result of Lake Erie being higher than Lake Ontario and the draining water flowing over a rock cliff (below).

The Rocky and Appalachian Mountains were formed at different times during the flood (left).

Coal does not have to be formed over long periods of time. The petrified tree in the center of the photo extends through a coal bed and surrounding rock layers. The layers must have formed quickly or the tree would have rotted.

How Long Does It Take to Form Petrified Wood?

Petrified wood can form, under laboratory conditions, in a very short period of time. There are even companies who produce petrified wood commercially to be used in real "hardwood floors."

There are many examples of wood petrifying in a short period of time. A wooden board dangled in the hot silica-rich waters of a hot spring in Yellowstone was substantially petrified in one year.

The speed of petrifaction is related to the pressures which inject the hot silica-rich waters into the wood. Silica surrounds or replaces each cell, thereby turning the entire wooden object into solid stone.

How Are Stalactites and Stalagmites Formed?

Most caves are found in limestone. The calcium carbonate present in limestone easily dissolves in ground water. The warmer the water and the higher the acidity, the greater the amount of calcium carbonate which can be dissolved by the water.

When water saturated with calcium carbonate enters an open space such as a cave, it cools off or evaporates, leaving the calcium carbonate behind. Stalactites (holding "tightly" to the ceiling) and stalagmites (which are usually larger and thus more "mighty" than stalactites) are formed as this calcium carbonate precipitates out of the water.

Cave formations are the result of water evaporating and depositing calcium carbonate.

Obviously, the rate of precipitation varies with the amount of water, the temperature, the acidity, other chemicals present, etc. In many modern caves, the conditions are not conducive to rapid growth of precipitates, leading to the tale that it takes long periods of time to build up large stalactites and stalagmites. In other cases, where the conditions are better, both have been seen to grow quite rapidly, sometimes totally enclosing human artifacts or animals. Stalactites or stalagmites have even been seen to form in structures, such as the basements of buildings, under bridges, and in mines. Some of the huge features in major caves, however, give evidence that conditions were even more favorable in the past. One can surmise that recently deposited sediments saturated with warm and acidic flood water would have been just right for the rapid growth of such cave features.

How Is Coal Formed?

It is usually thought that coal is formed as a layer of organic peat accumulates in the bottom of a swamp, later to be submerged under the ocean and buried by ocean bottom sediments. Millions of years of heat and pressure are thought to be required.

Actually, the features found in modern peat are totally unlike the features found in coal, and nowhere on earth is peat seen to change into coal. Coal can be formed in a laboratory by heating organic material away from oxygen but in the presence of volcanic clay. Under such conditions, coal can be formed in a matter of hours.

One wonders if the abundant forest growing before the flood would not have formed huge log mats floating on the flood ocean. As these decayed and were buried by hot sediments in the presence of volcanic clay, they might have rapidly turned to coal. A situation very analogous to that happened at Mount St. Helens following the eruption of 1980.

Coal could have been formed by huge layers of floating trees that were buried during the flood. A situation similar to this occurred with large log jams being created by the eruption of Mount St. Helens in 1980.

How Is Natural Gas Formed?

Natural gas, mostly methane, is given off in the coalification process. Large commercial quantities of methane also occur near where oil is found.

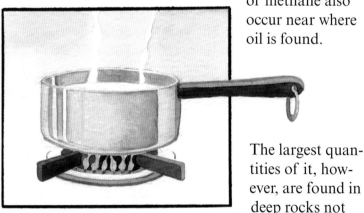

The natural gas that powers the stoves and heaters in many homes usually comes from underground.

The largest quantities of it, however, are found in deep rocks not associated with decomposition of organic material. Methane (CH_4) is a rather simple molecule. It is also found in the gases given off by volcanic eruptions, and occasionly in meteorites. Evidently, some natural gas is from both organic and inorganic sources.

How Is Oil Formed?

Coal is obviously the altered remains of plant material. Organic natural gas is from the decomposition of both plant and animal remains as well as a product of the digestive systems of animals and man.

Many theories have been promoted as to the specific origin of oil. The best seems to be that it is the remains of algae once floating in the ocean but buried in ocean sediments. Oil is not the remains of dinosaurs as has sometimes been claimed.

Are Dinosaur Fossils the Most Abundant Type of Fossil?

Thousands of pieces of dinosaur fossils have been found and certainly there are thousands more waiting to be found, but actually dinosaur fossils are quite rare. They are found on every continent, but just in a few places.

Most fossils are of sea creatures, fish, and insects. Only relatively few fossils are of land animals. Dinosaurs, being reptiles, probably had a slightly higher fossilization potential than did mammals during the devastating waters of the flood, but not nearly as much potential as marine animals such as clams.

Dinosaur fossils such as the T-Rex above are actually quite rare.

Chapter 8

THE FUTURE EARTH

A s remarkable as the origin, the past, and the present of the earth have been, the future will be even more remarkable.

In the original earth, the rains were restrained, but the abundant crops were watered from continual sources of mist and water springing up from below. Many creation scientists believe that protective water vapor surrounding the earth produced ideal conditions worldwide. Even after Adam's sin ruined creation, some individuals lived for almost a thousand years.

Once sin entered into the creation, it was no longer perfect, but remained a wonderful place in which to live until the flood. When sin had reached its unacceptable high, God judged the world and restructured it through a watery devastation. Ever since then, we have lived in a flooded and cursed remnant of that once-beautiful world.

Many scholars believe that the Bible teaches that, unfortunately, things on earth will get worse before they get better. They see biblical prophecies telling of a coming period of time during which the world will once again be convulsed by God's judgment. An intense heat wave will be coupled with a scorching drought causing great famine on earth. Flaming objects, possibly comets, will crash into

As part of God's judgment for disobedience at the end of time, the earth will undergo heat waves, droughts, flaming comets, earthquakes and plagues.

the sea, earthquakes will remove mountains, and plagues will devastate humanity.

But then, when the time is just right, the Creator will return to complete the judgment and restore the world. Christ himself will set up His Kingdom and will reign on earth.

When the Creator came to earth before, He lived in the cursed world and in the presence of sinful man. He had come to live a sinless life and die as a perfect sacrifice for the sins of His rebellious creation. He set in motion His plan of full restoration of the earth to its original created intent.

Many responded to Him and accepted His free gift of forgiveness, salvation, and eternal life, but many others rejected Him. This is the nature of man, for even now, in spite of all the evidence, they still reject Him and will continue to do so. What

When Christ came to the earth the first time, He died on the cross and arose from the grave in His plan to redeem the earth from its curse of sin. When He returns again, He will restore the earth to the conditions before the fall of man.

follows will be His ultimate judgment and their eternal banishment from His presence.

The New Earth

"The heavens shall pass away with a great noise, and the elements shall melt with fervent heat, the earth also and the works that are therein shall be burned up. . . .the coming of the day of God, wherein the heavens being on fire shall be dissolved, and the elements shall melt with fervent heat. Nevertheless we, according to His promise, look for a new heavens and a new earth, wherein dwelleth righteousness" (2 Pet. 3:10-13)

This present earth will be completely melted and re-created. No longer will we experience or even be reminded of bad things. No more volcanoes or earthquakes or storms. Even the fossils and sedimentary rock will be no more, for they are the results of the flood of Noah's day and death as the penalty for sin. The entire universe will be pure and righteousness will be welcome.

This wonderful new earth promises to be beyond our imagination in its beauty and perfection. From the hints we have in Scripture it will be very similar to the Garden of Eden before Adam and Eve rebelled. "And God Himself shall be with them, and be their God. And God shall wipe away all tears from their eyes; and there shall be no more death, neither sorrow, nor crying, neither shall there be any more pain: for the former things are passed away. And he who sat upon the throne said, 'Behold I make all things new' " (Rev. 21:3–5).

Those who have rejected His free gift of salvation "shall be punished with everlasting destruction from the presence of the Lord, and from the glory of His power" (2 Thess. 1:9). The righteous Judge "shall cast them into the furnace of fire; there shall be wailing and gnashing of teeth" (Matt. 13:50).

Eternity Awaits

Where will you be throughout eternity? Will you be in the glorious new earth experiencing His fellowship and grace forever? Or, will you be in the fires of outer darkness experiencing His wrath, banished from His presence forever? "All have sinned and come short of the glory of God" (Rom. 3:23).

Those who have acknowledged their sin, repented of it, and gone to the Creator/Savior for forgiveness will receive that forgiveness and be assured of eternal life and a home in the new earth.

That new earth will be characterized by righteousness (2 Pet. 3:13). Sinners will not be present, but those who have been declared righteous will be there, "being justified freely by His grace through the redemption that is in Christ Jesus" (Rom. 3:24).

If we believe that Jesus Christ, the Creator, God the Son, died on the cross to pay the penalty for our sins, and if we repent of those sins and ask Him to forgive us for those sins, we will be declared righteous and will dwell with Him forever in that new earth.

The old earth will be destroyed by God in a fervent heat, but He will create a new earth in which there will be no more pain or death. God himself will rule this new world.

BIBLIOGRAPHY

Ager, Derek. *The New Catastrophism.* Press Syndicate of the Cambridge University Press, 1993.

Austin, Steven A. Ph.D. *Mount St. Helen's Field Study Tour.* Santee, CA: Institute for Creation Research, 1999.

Austin, Steven A. Ph.D. *Catastrophe Data Base.* Santee, CA: Institute for Creation Research, 2000

Austin, Steven A. Ph.D. *Yellowstone Field Study Tour.* Santee, CA: Institute for Creation Research, 2000

Beus, Stanley S. & Michael Morales. *Grand Canyon Geology.* New York Oxford University Press, Museum of Northern Arizona Press, 1990.

Brand, Leonard. *Faith, Reason, & Earth History.* Berrien Springs, MI: Andrews University Press, 1997.

Chronic, Halka. *Roadside Geology of Arizona.* Mountain Press Publishing Company, 1989.

Coffin, Harold with Robert H. Brown. *Origin by Design.* Hagerstown, MD: Review and Herald Publishing Association, 1983.

Decker, Robert & Barbara Decker. *Volcanoes.* San Francisco, CA: W. H. Freeman & Co.,1981.

Foster, Robert J. *Geology.* second edition. Columbus, OH: Charles E. Merrill Publishing Co., 1966, 1971.

Harris, Ann G. *Geology of National Parks.* third edition. Dubuque, IA: Kendall/Hunt Publishing Company.

Lewis, Douglas W. & David McConchie. *Practical Sedimentology.* NY: Chapman & Hall, 1994.

Morris, Henry M. Ph.D. *The Biblical Basis for Modern Science.* Grand Rapids, MI: Baker Book House, 1984.

Roth, Ariel A. *Origins: Linking Science and Scripture*, Review and Herald Publishing Association, 1998.

Rothery, David A. *Teach Yourself Geology.* London: Hodder Headline Plc, 1997.

Walsh, Robert E. *International Conference on Creationism, Technical Symposium Sessions.* Pittsburgh, PA: Creation Science Fellowship, Inc., 1998.

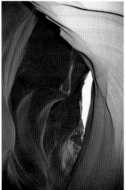

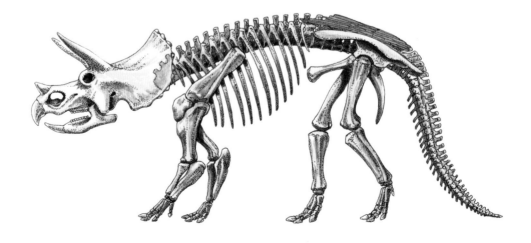

RESOURCES

Resources on the general subject of geology, the global flood of Noah's day, and creation.

BOOKS

1. *Noah's Ark, Noah's Flood: Lots of Water, Lots of Mud* by John D. Morris, (Green Forest, AR: Master Books, 1998), 32 p. (for young readers).

2. *Noah's Ark and the Ararat Adventure* by John D. Morris, (Green Forest, AR: Master Books, 1994), 62 p. (for 7th grade to adult).

3. *Life in the Great Ice Age* by Michael & Beverly Oard, (Green Forest, AR: Master Books, 1993) 72 p. (for 4th grade to adult).

4. *The Young Earth* by John D. Morris, (Green Forest, AR: Master Books, 1994), 206 p. (for high school to adult).

5. *The Modern Creation Trilogy* by Henry M. Morris and John D. Morris, (Green Forest, AR: Master Books, 1996), 774 p. (for interested laymen).

6. *Grand Canyon: Monument to Catastrophe* edited by Steve Austin (Santee, CA: Institute for Creation Research, 1994), 284 p. (college level science).

VIDEOS

1. *The Creation Adventure Series* — for young children (Santee, CA: Institute for Creation Research, 1999)
   a. *Marty's Fossil Adventure*
   b. *Marty and the Last Dinosaur*

2. *A Walk Through History* — A tour of the Institute for Creation Research's Museum of Creation and Earth History with Dr. John D. Morris (Santee, CA: Institute for Creation Research, 1994)

3. *The Grand Canyon Catastrophe* — shows how the Grand Canyon was eroded (Keziah Video Productions, 1996)

4. *The Deluge* — Dr. John Morris discusses the great flood of Noah's day from Mt. Ararat in Turkey (Santee, CA: Institute for Creation Research, 1993)

5. *Mount St. Helens: Explosive Evidence for Creation* — with Dr. Steve Austin (Santee, CA: Institute for Creation Research, 1989)

PHOTO CREDITS

l=left; r=right; c=center; t=top; b=bottom; a=all

Bryan Miller 7, 8t, 8bl, 9br, 14tr, 14b, 16tr, 17tr, 17cr, 19b, 21tr, 21tc, 21cr, 23t, 25a, 26cr, 27t, 28b, 29b, 31b, 32t, 34t, 37r, 42b, 44b, 45b, 47t, 48, 49, 50, 51c, 53t, 54b, 55, 56, 57, 58br, 59, 60t, 60b, 61, 70tc, 72, 73b, 74, 75

Institute for Creation Research 10bl, 11br, 15tl, 16tl, 16bl, 17tl, 24b, 30b, 31t, 34c, 35t, 36a, 38t, 38bl, 39c, 39br, 40a, 41cl, 42tr, 43tl, 44t, 46b, 51b, 52b, 53b, 69bl, 70br, 71tl, 72t

N.O.A.A. & NGDC 9t, 20cl, 22t, 35c, 35b, 42l, 43r, 44br, 45br, 45t, 46t, 47b, 70tl, 71tl

U.S.G.S. 9c, 11t, 12t, 17br, 18bl, 21cl, 24t, 68

Scenic America vol. 50 CD 5, 6t, 10t, 12b, 20t, 20b, 22b, 23c, 26l, 26b, 27c, 28t, 29tl, 29tr, 33, 37b, 54t, 58t, 69r, 69t, 73t

Master Books 6c, 9bl, 10c, 11c, 11bl, 13a, 14l, 14r, 15tr, 15c, 17cl, 17b, 18cl, 18t, 18r, 19t, 19c, 30t, 39t, 41r, 58bl, 60c, 64, 65, 66, 67, 70br, 72br

Cosmic Cavern; Berryville, Arkansas 15br, 70br

NASA 4, 32b, 66t

Astronomy and Space CD 6b, 8br

GLOSSARY

Basalt — A type of igneous rock that makes up most of the oceanic crust. On land it forms when extruded by volcanoes or through fissures.

Catastrophism — The philosophy about the past, which allows for totally different processes and/or different process rates, scales, and intensities than those operating today. Includes the idea that processes such as creation and dynamic global flooding have shaped the entire planet.

Chemical rock — A type of sedimentary rock built up as chemicals in water, usually seawater, precipitate and consolidate.

Clastic rock — A type of sedimentary rock consisting of fragments of a previously existing rock (i.e., sandstone consists of consolidated sand grains).

Continental separation — The concept that the continental plates have moved apart (or collided), concluding, for example, that Africa and South America were once connected.

Core — The center of the earth is thought to be a sphere of iron and nickel, divided into two zones. The outer core is in molten or liquid form, while the inner core is solid.

Crust — The thin covering of planet Earth, which includes the continents and ocean basins. Nowhere is it more than 60 miles (100 km) thick .

Fault — A fracture in rock along which separation or movement has taken place.

Fold — A bend or flexure in a layer of rock.

Fossil — The direct or indirect remains of an animal or plant.

Granite — A widespread igneous rock, which contains abundant quartz and feldspar, and makes up a significant portion of the continental crust.

Igneous rock — Rock formed when hot, molten magma cools and solidifies.

Mantle — Beneath the thin crust and above the core of the earth. It is about 1,864 miles (3,000 km) thick.

Metamorphic rock — Rocks formed when heat, pressure, and/or chemical action alters previously existing rock.

Plate — The earth's crust, both continental and oceanic, is divided into plates, with boundaries identified by zones of earthquake activity. The idea of plate tectonics holds that these plates move relative to one another, sometimes separating or colliding, and sometimes moving past each other.

Radioisotope Dating — The attempt to determine a rock's age by measuring the ratio of radioactive isotopes and the rate at which they decay.

Sedimentary rock — Rock formed by the deposition and consolidation of loose particles of sediment, and those formed by precipitation from water.

Tsunami — Often called a tidal wave. A seismic sea wave produced by an underwater disturbance such as an earthquake, volcano or landslide. Can be extremely destructive.

Uniformitarianism — The philosophy about the past which assumes no past events of a different nature than those possible today, and/or operating at rates, scales and intensities far greater than those operating today. The slogan "the present is the key to the past" characterizes this idea.

INDEX

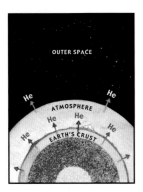